BFI TV Classics

BFI TV Classics is a series of books celebrating key ı̣ ....evision programmes and series. Television scholars, critics and nu.....sts provide critical readings underpinned with careful research, alongside a personal response to the programme and a case for its 'classic' status

Also Published:

Buffy the Vampire Slayer
Anne Billson

Doctor Who
Kim Newman

Our Friends in the North
Michael Eaton

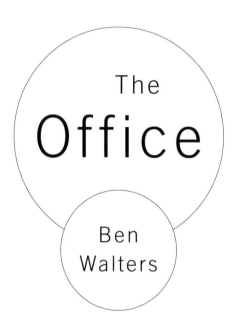

The
Office

Ben
Walters

 Publishing

First published in 2005 by the
British Film Institute
21 Stephen Street, London W1T 1LN

The British Film Institute's purpose is to champion moving image culture in all its richness and diversity across the UK, for the benefit of as wide an audience as possible, and to create and encourage debate.

British Library Cataloguing-in-Publication Data
A catalogue record for this book is available from the British Library

ISBN 1-84457-091-6

Set by Fakenham Photosetting Ltd, Fakenham, Norfolk
Printed in the UK by Butler and Tanner Ltd, Frome, Somerset

NB Episodes of *The Office* are referred to in the form I.i (for series one, episode one), II.v (for series two, episode five) etc. Unless alternative reference is given, quotations from Ricky Gervais, Stephen Merchant, Ash Atalla, Anil Gupta, Jon Plowman and Jane Root are taken from interviews with the author.

Contents

Introduction

In the weeks prior to the first transmission of *The Office* in July 2001, British situation comedy did not seem to offer much hope of excellence. Several new BBC shows had failed to secure recommissions and the Corporation's comedy department was widely perceived as being in crisis. 'Is this the end for TV sitcoms?' asked the *Daily Mail*;[1] 'Something is rotten in the state of TV comedy', claimed the *Daily Telegraph*;[2] the *Guardian* suggested the genre had 'Both feet in the grave'.[3] On paper, the series that was about to launch on BBC2 scarcely seemed a likely remedy: created and performed by unknowns, it was conspicuously banal in its setting and offered nothing in the way of elaborate plotting or farcical mishap, punchlines or catchphrases. Even its own characters were stultified with boredom, when they weren't cringing in embarrassment. Yet *The Office* would become the BBC's most talked-about sitcom in years, win dozens of domestic and international awards, break sales records on DVD and eventually be sold to over sixty countries and remade for American audiences. How did the frustrations and aspirations of a bunch of clerical workers at a paper merchants in Slough ever catch on?

One way of approaching that question would be to look at the failed series that had prompted such negative press attention: there was the tame *The Savages*, which tried to apply a slick, machine-tooled American approach to a British family sitcom; *Office Gossip*, starring Pauline Quirke, which used the workplace as the basis for conventionally heightened sitcom larks; *Lee Evans – So What Now?*, a star vehicle as bereft of direction as its title suggests. Where these were ingratiating, with a premium on famous performers and traditional farce structure, *The Office*'s painful plausibility, though initially unpalatable, offered provocative characterisation and emotional engagement; where the high-profile series had been loaded with disproportionate expectations of delivering critical and popular success from the start, *The Office* could not have opened with less fanfare, its gradual 'discovery' by both viewers and critics arguably compounding the programme's emotional resonance with an affectionate feeling of ownership. As some of those newspaper articles suggested, conventional genre sitcom was being outstripped by shows like *The Royle Family* (BBC2, 1998–2000), whose naturalistic aesthetic delivered situations and behaviour with which viewers could identify – even if, in the case of *The Office*, that identification often took the form of discomfort.

Unlike most television workplaces, the office of *The Office* is an unusually faithful representation of the clerical environment, with particular attention to the low-level enervation resulting from the lack of privacy in the open-plan layout. Nowhere is this more acutely expressed than in the character of David Brent, the middle manager who exploits his limited authority to promote his deluded conception of himself as an inspirational 'chilled-out entertainer'. Brent wants not simply to be liked, but to be appreciated for talents whose absence is plain to all but himself. To see a man labouring through an endeavour whose failure is obvious to everyone else is embarrassing; when that endeavour is the provocation of laughter it becomes mortifying; when one is directly implicated in the situation it can be almost unbearable. *The Office*'s co-option of the docusoap aesthetic was not just a means of enhancing its sustained naturalism (although it achieved this to great effect): it also made the presence of the camera an acknowledged and integral part of the set-up, with the result that when Brent shows off, he isn't just showing off to those around him, but to the camera, and therefore directly to *us*. It's much harder to laugh at a ridiculous situation if one has a personal investment in its outcome, and *The Office* goes to great lengths to reduce the distance between action and audience: much of this is achieved through its plausible realism, but it's Brent's persistent, approval-seeking attention to the lens that really turns the screw by locating us within the dynamic we're observing.

For, if *The Office* is a situation comedy, it's worth considering just what that situation is. Superficially, it's the experience of the contemporary white-collar workplace, where often tedious activity goes hand in hand with underlying insecurity about one's employment status – a newly pervasive and disaffecting combination of ennui and anxiety that has gone relatively unnoticed by television writers. But other aspects of the show – the dominating presence of the camera, the attention to the modes of representation and behaviour associated with the docusoap form – point towards another fundamental situation, one that links the contemporary worker's vulnerable status with contemporary television's fascination with 'reality': the state of being observed. In addition to the self-monitoring necessitated by the circumstances of the open-plan office, most of *The Office*'s characters are to some degree revealed through their relationship with the lens. Of course, it's Brent who places the highest premium on its approval, constantly (if inefficiently) monitoring the impression he makes. His familiarity with TV – from its stock catchphrases to its production methods – and his aspiration to the status of professional entertainer confirm *The Office* as a television comedy about television and about comedy.

It would be inaccurate, however, to view the show as an echoing exercise in postmodern referentiality simply making play with the acknowledged fact of recording. Rather, it takes self-consciousness as fundamental to its circumstances and then offers an empathetic engagement with characters obliged to operate under its yoke, from the achingly incremental progression of Tim and Dawn's flirtation to the painful disintegration of Brent's own character. Ultimately Brent's dependence on the approval of the lens renders him less ridiculous than pathetic, and therefore sympathetic. When he quotes from John Betjeman's poem 'Slough', Brent understandably omits the following stanzas:

3

And get that man with double chin
Who'll always cheat and always win,
Who washes his repulsive skin
In women's tears:

And smash his desk of polished oak
And smash his hands so used to stroke
And stop his boring dirty joke
And make him yell.

But spare the bald young clerks who add
The profits of the stinking cad;
It's not their fault that they are mad,
They've tasted Hell.

That man with double chin

There is a whiff of hell about the offices of Wernham Hogg, the suspicion articulated by Sartre in *Huis Clos* that 'L'enfer, c'est les autres' ('Hell is other people') – not a misanthropic dismissal but the recognition that our inevitably partial and distorted expressions can only leave us with flawed conceptions of ourselves and others through which we must nevertheless struggle to make communion. 'Il existe une quantité de gens dans le monde qui sont en enfer parce qu'ils dépendent trop du jugement d'autrui,' Sartre said: some people condemn themselves to hell through their dependence on the judgment of others. Perhaps the finest achievement of *The Office* is its demonstration that though he cheats, strokes, tells dirty jokes, that man with double chin is the least able to show empathy and the neediest of it, not the diabolical tormentor he seems but the damnedest of them all – yet gifted, in the end, a glimpse of salvation.

5

Origins

The creators of *The Office* met in an office. In 1997, Ricky Gervais, Head of Speech at the fledgling London radio station XFM, hired Stephen Merchant as his assistant and they immediately established the rapport that would be their basic work mode, whether in the XFM show they would later host together or when they came to start writing together. As Gervais recalls in interview,

> The first time we met we talked like we've just been talking now, quoting Billy Wilder to each other or 'Don't you hate it when – ? Did you see so-and-so? Fucking disgrace. He can't act.' That was seven hours out of our day and then two minutes 'I'll tell you what someone said to me once –' 'Oh, we'll have that [as material].'

Gervais's stint at XFM didn't last beyond the station's acquisition by Capital Radio in 1998. As David Brent later would, Gervais used his unanticipated redundancy to pursue his ambitions as an entertainer; Merchant, meanwhile, had taken a place on the BBC's Trainee Assistant Producer Scheme (TAPS). It was during his stint there that Merchant came into contact with BBC Head of Entertainment Paul Jackson and Head of Comedy Entertainment Jon Plowman. He also worked on *Comedy Nation* (1998–9) – a short-lived BBC2 sketch show intended to foster new production and performing talent – where he met Ash Atalla, who had moved from work experience on *Watchdog* (1986–) to various junior research jobs, before securing a comedy assignment from Plowman. The show provided both with their first sustained experience of comedy production.

The TAPS programme also required the production of a short feature. 'Normally you do something serious about the drug trade in Bristol or homelessness in Aberdeen,' Plowman notes, but Merchant decided to shoot Gervais as 'Seedy Boss' – a character Gervais had developed more or less to entertain people down the pub – though he had never acted for the camera before. Made in June 1998, the twenty-minute short featured him as David Brent (the name was already decided), managing director of a wood-pulp bleach-and-dye business in Staffordshire. Shot at Gervais's old office at the University of London Union, where he had worked as entertainment officer for eight years, it was of necessity a basic undertaking. 'That was just us and a couple of friends,' says Gervais, 'some people who actually were still working at ULU.' The authentic appearance of the workplace environment on show was therefore down to the fact that it actually was a functioning office.

'We shot it in the documentary style because that was the quickest way to do it,' Merchant recalls.

> We only had a camera crew on the day, so we decided to do it that way because it would forgive any kind of dodgy lighting or noise or clunks, and just meant we could do it a lot quicker. We also realised that if we interviewed the character we could get more stuff in the can without lots of lengthy set-ups.

This approach had formal consequences as well as practical benefits: 'because Ricky was playing the character as completely as he could, he realised he had to play it with the knowledge that he was showing off to the camera, because that's what this character would

7

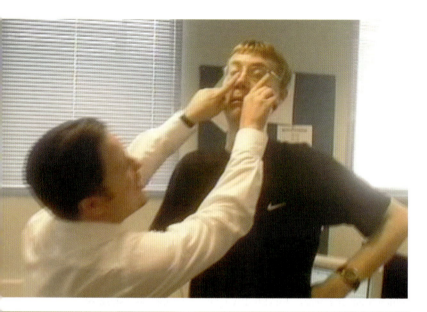

Seedy boss: Gervais with Merchant and Nicola Cotter in the TAPS short

have done.' Thus the complicity between subject and camera was also fundamental from the start, although the camera is a less obvious presence here than it would become in the series proper. Even so, the receptionist character gives a conspicuous double-take when she spots the camera and Gervais glances at it on several occasions, though without the lingering engagement that would become Brent's trademark. Gervais says that 'probably the single biggest influence on *The Office* would have been *This Is Spinal Tap* (1983) – a fake documentary but very realistic and about little bits and pieces.'

Gratingly jovial and convinced of his own talents as both manager and entertainer with 'the gift of laughter', Brent was basically the same character viewers of *The Office* would come to know a couple of years later; indeed much of the material from this taster would find its way more or less unchanged into the series' first episode, from individual lines ('el vino did flow') to whole scenes, from the first – in which Brent engineers a forklift driving job for a man as a show of power – to the last, in which his 'joke' sacking of his receptionist (here called June) backfires horribly. We see him engaged in misjudged banter with his receptionist that turns unexpectedly aggressive; using a tour for a new temp, Ricky, as a peg for his routines; employing a new secretary, Karen Roper, by means of a sleazy, queasy interview (as in I.v); and showing off in talking heads ('People say I'm the best boss. They go to me: "We've never worked in a place like this. You're such a laugh. You get the best out of us." And I go: "C'est la vie. If that's true, excellent." ').

Among the differences between this venture and the series it would later spawn is the office layout itself, which was less open than Wernham Hogg's, allowing for less interaction between characters. There's also a certain neatness to the plot, which sees receptionist June playing a relatively harmless prank on Ricky before her own 'sacking', which ends more harshly than the comparable scene in I.i, with June accusing Brent of being an unbalanced pervert and him growing explicitly irate and misogynist

9

('if I *was* mad, I'd slap the slut'). Merchant also appears as 'the office joker – stand-up comedian' – an occupation Merchant was indeed trying at the time, though here he proves merely the subject of Brent's enervating jocularity. There's also more explicit docusoap-style apparatus, including an introductory voice-over read by Merchant, whose voice is also heard in the talking-head sequences.

Merchant's contacts in the BBC comedy department ensured this twenty-minute tape was soon in circulation, although he received little initial encouragement. However, Merchant's old acquaintance Ash Atalla – now a junior TV comedy producer with Radio 4's disability-based sketch show, *Yes Sir, I Can Boogie* (1999–2000), to his name – recalls that 'when I saw Ricky do David Brent I thought that was brilliant . . . the twitches of his face, the small movements of his eye.' Sensing that he might have found a project with the potential to be his own breakthrough as a producer, Atalla approached Merchant.

10

I remember saying to Stephen: 'The way our random industry works, especially within a big organisation like the BBC, you really need someone to champion an idea' . . . I was twenty-seven, with no real track record, so it wasn't like they had acquired a producer with a lot of clout. But at the same time it wasn't like I had [hit the jackpot], because who were these guys?

After receiving a cool reception from Head of Comedy Entertainment, Jon Plowman, Atalla contacted established BBC comedy producer Anil Gupta for his opinion. 'Anil was riding very high on *Goodness Gracious Me* (1998–2000), which was at the height of its powers then,' Atalla recalls, referring to the highly successful sketch show which Gupta had produced. Gupta viewed the tape and agreed to join Atalla in trying to get it produced. Gupta recalls:

I went to see Jon [Plowman] with the tape again and said: 'I think it's great and we should definitely make a pilot at least'. Now he'll dispute this, 'cause he's disputed it to me since, but it's definitely true. He said: 'Well, okay, if you say so. But he [Gervais] can't be the lead.' And I said: 'You're insane, he's the show.' He said: 'He's too unlikeable a character, you wouldn't believe he'd ever be in that position.'

Plowman's recollections are indeed different, though he admits to finding the tape challenging. 'I remember saying to Ricky very early on: "Why isn't this guy sacked for being completely useless?" And he looked at me and said: "Look around you" – meaning Television Centre. "People don't get sacked for being useless." ' Still, Plowman claims to have been sufficiently intrigued to offer his support. 'It's usually those things where you go: "I've no idea where this is going" that are the really interesting things. There's no point saying: "That's not like every other comedy we've ever made." That's probably the reason for making it.'

In any case, Gupta's coming on board had provided a bridge between the junior writers and producer and the upper echelons of the BBC. Given Gervais', Merchant's and his own inexperience, Atalla was sympathetic to Plowman's hesitiation, noting that 'Anil was the safety blanket for Jon, and us. He was the only one that knew anything!'

While interest at the BBC gradually grew, Merchant and Gervais had created a half-hour pilot for Channel 4's experimental *Comedy Lab* (1998–2005) strand. 'Golden Years', broadcast in September 1999, occupies similar territory to *The Office*, based as it is on the absurd desire of a hopelessly untalented office manager to be a professional entertainer. Gervais plays the joint owner of a successful video rental chain, Clive, who nurses an obsessive ambition to appear as David Bowie on *Stars in Their Eyes* (1990–). Initially shown through chairing meetings in full Ziggy Stardust regalia, his aspirations eventually lead to an abortive parallel career as a lookalike. The parallels with Brent are clear, and enhanced by the character's crass insensitivity, anxiety over his age and 'celebrity status' (like Brent he

11

gets his ear pierced only to find 'It really stings') and frequent mangled attempts at self-clarification and self-promotion. Clive's long-suffering PA, Zoe, is rather like *The Office*'s Dawn while his business partner, Barry, foreshadows Neil in his snide, humourless professionalism. There are analogues too for the characters of Lee (Dawn's fiancé) and Finchy (Brent's ostensible best mate), as well as awkward silences and sustained, naturalistic attention to the banality of the office environment (a ruler and a hole punch are pivotal props). There's a foretaste too of some of *The Office*'s formal effects: Clive's audition tape provides the opportunity for direct, shifty interaction with the camera, including some 'pop-star' affectations. 'Golden Years' also hints at Gervais' enduring fascination with Bowie (they became friends after *The Office*'s success) and indeed his own short-lived pop career: Gervais' New Wave band, Seona Dancing, released two singles in the early 1980s.

The TAPS taster tape had also helped secure for Gervais a regular slot on Channel 4's distinctly patchy satirical series, *The 11 O'Clock Show* (1998–2000), the fourth series of which started the month after 'Golden Years' went out. Taking up the slot vacated by Sacha Baron Cohen's character Ali G, Gervais built on his XFM persona, offering topical commentary in a tongue-in-cheek mode based on prejudice and ignorance: 'If you're looking for informed, unbiased reflection on the day's news,' one introduction ran, 'you don't want Ricky Gervais.' Jokes in conspicuously bad taste about elderly, disabled, gay or foreign people – often childishly provocative rather than actually funny – were occasionally undercut by gags at his own expense that left Gervais staring helplessly into the camera; this use of clashing registers, the slippage between presentation and substance, was to become characteristic.

A similar combination of sarcastic bigotry and attention to the circumstances of production would characterise *Come Together with Ricky Gervais* (2000), for satellite channel UK Play, which saw Gervais (with an embarrassing spiky haircut) introducing music videos from a brick-walled warehouse-cum-living room rather like the loft apartment where the video for Brent's own self-financed single is set. Along with jokes at the expense of gays or foreigners, there was the usual slightly guarded interaction with the camera: after getting tangled up Gervais might say 'We'll do that in the edit, that'll be fine'; ad breaks were sometimes used to 'interrupt' dodgy anecdotes; and at one point he advises an unseen runner that 'It's good to start off on a poxy channel that doesn't matter like UK Play or whatever it's called 'cause no one knows what they're doing . . . or they're bent.'

The *11 O'Clock Show* appearances led to a talk-show series for Channel 4, *Meet Ricky Gervais*, which ran in September and October 2000. Boasting the usual semi-offensive broadsides ('For those of you who are thinking of complaining,' Gervais said as he signed off from the last episode, 'don't forget in this series we've covered the French, the Special Olympics, famine, flooding, Thora Hird and div kids'), the show also featured interviews with guests from old-school television, such as John Virgo, Jimmy Savile and Peter Purves,[4] and weekly pastiches of vintage game shows. *Meet Ricky Gervais* also demonstrated continued attention to the production process: audience participation items went deliberately wrong, while the opening consisted of a technical countdown ident over which we heard Gervais being chastised by a 'producer'[5] for his puerile amateurism in failing to secure credits or a theme tune. Most interesting were 'backstage' segments in which Gervais appeared not as a cocky bigot showing off to the camera but a demure, blank-faced naïf subject to the abusive attentions and sexual exploitation of an unnamed channel executive, creepily played by Merchant, who arranged for their encounters to be recorded. Recording technology was central to this weird melange of vulnerability and complicity, but out of Gervais' control: he looks humbly up at a CCTV camera, allows a photographer to shoot him masturbating and, in the last episode, is sexually humiliated in front of the audience in the main studio.

Meanwhile, Merchant and Gervais' twenty-minute taster tape had not been forgotten at the BBC. As an audiovisual sketch, it gave a much greater idea of the set-up's potential than was usual for a comedy

13

proposal; indeed, without Gervais' performance the concept was distinctly uninspiring. 'On the face of it, if you go down the boxes we tick with *The Office*, it's almost like we were trying to not give it an audience,' Gervais says.

> Let's not have any real jokes, let's not have any catchphrases, let's have no one dressing up in wigs and acting funnily, let's not have a laughter track, let's have nothing happen, let's make everyone a little bit bored, let's make no one actually funny. It was like it was the antichrist of comedy.

The tape alone was still not enough to secure a commission but Jon Plowman now believed it was at least worth pitching to BBC controller Jane Root as a potential pilot, so, he recalls, 'I gave them some money to go away and develop a script.'

Gupta and Atalla began discussing with Gervais and Merchant how to develop their character study into something with sitcom potential. Gupta recalls:

> *Seinfeld* was coming to the end of its life but still looked at as quite a big show, and there was lots of that sort of myth of *Seinfeld*, that it's about nothing. Ricky and Steve were keen on it being just scenes from an office – you know, offices are boring and nothing happens and that's what it's like because it's real. And Jon and I were very much of the opinion that that's all well and good but I don't want to spend half an hour of my life watching that on telly if I work in one. There's got to be a story.

Such suggestions weren't always initially welcomed, even if they later became integral to the script. 'Ricky and Steve are extremely talented and very bright blokes but their first reaction to being told something is to say: "Fuck off",' Gupta says.

But having said that, they're not stupid, so they tend to go away and think about it and then quite often it happens and it's never really acknowledged that it's happened. But we said: 'Look, there really has to be a story, and you want some kind of through line within an episode and across the series as well, probably.' There'd also been through the late 90s the whole *Friends* Ross-and-Rachel [continuing plot] and that really works, hooks people in.

Merchant and Gervais, however, maintain that narrative was key to their conception of *The Office* from the start.

It's odd [Anil] remembers us battling with them over story arcs and plot. We'd had conversations about stories and the need for narrative and how the show would unfold long before we ever had meetings at the BBC. We brought up the idea of doing a Ross and Rachel-style romance and it was something we were excited about from the beginning. I think what scared them was that we were fighting against writing traditional wacky sitcom storylines. We were trying to find a way of disguising the plots so that they didn't undermine the realism, so that you wouldn't see the narrative mechanics at work. We wanted the illusion that you were merely watching scenes from an office but that they were actually building up into a picture of the world, becoming more than the sum of their parts.

15

The transition from character study to fully fledged situation comedy also required a more sustained engagement with the faux-docusoap style. This was something Merchant and Gervais were keen to retain, with 'an absolute love of realism' as key motivator for Gervais: 'there's nothing funnier than real life, real documentaries. They resonate more.' The taster had initially plumped for such an approach, Merchant acknowledges,

for the sake of ease, but [having] done it like that we had to obey the rules of documentary – and the rules of documentary are that everyone acts up to [the camera] and everyone's conscious of it. So when we

wrote the series everything always had to be geared around 'how are
they acting, where's the camera, are they conscious of it, have they
forgotten about it at this moment?'

After flirting with genre spoof, it was decided to play the form straight;
it would be a means of exploring character and situation rather than the
basis for jokes about incompetent film-making.

　　The writing process took several months but proved worth the
wait. 'They came back with this script and it was like "They've done
it!" ' Gupta recalls. Atalla was equally impressed.

I remember reading it and suddenly there was Gareth, suddenly there
was Tim and Dawn. What was exciting was you could see the love and
care and detail that had gone into David Brent had been multiplied by
four for these other main characters. And having seen Ricky's
performance on the taster tape then we thought: 'Well, if we can get
the others to be that good then we could be onto something.'

Gupta was also pleased to see strong narrative strands in place. The
romantic potential of Tim and Dawn's relationship was perhaps more
implicit than obvious, but the addition of Brent's boss Jennifer Taylor
Clarke, and the threat of branch closure added an immediate sense of
jeopardy. 'They'd done all those things that they said they weren't going
to do but actually they'd done them rather brilliantly. It was all in the
first script really, almost from the first draft.'

　　Having delivered a viable script, senior BBC approval was
required for further progress. As Plowman explains,

Once every three or four months there's a thing called 'offers', when
both in-house [departments] and independent companies go to various
BBC heads of commissioning and channel controllers and say: 'Look,
we're offering you these things, do you want any of them?'

16

The Office became one of the proposals Plowman chose to pitch to the BBC2 controller at his next offers round [around June/July of 2000]. Atalla recalls the occasion.

> It was one of those big, almost clichéd meetings in a mahogany-lined room in the BBC, with Jane Root and all her people from the channel – her marketing people, her scheduler, her finance person – sitting down one end of a large oak table and me, Anil, Jon Plowman and Paul Jackson, who was head of the entertainment department, all sitting down at the other. It's quite a combative sort of thing, you're pitching aggressively – the comedy department have about seven or eight projects they want to pitch to the controller and the controller only has slots for one or two.

Aware that on paper *The Office* was a hard sell – 'This unknown guy called Ricky Gervais in a Slough office,' as Atalla puts it, 'and not a lot happens, and it's a fairly dowdy office' – the producers included highlights from the taster tape as part of their presentation. Gupta recalls:

17

> We said: 'Okay, we're going to come to this pitch meeting and we're going to need a TV and video.' And they said: 'Fine, no problem.' We turned up; there wasn't one. So I had to run down to my office, get my TV and video – this is in the BBC! – carry it up the stairs and plug it in. Jane watched it and then turned to her scheduler, Liam Keelan, and said: 'Is that funny?' And he went: 'Yes!' And she went: 'Oh, okay.' So they said: 'All right, well, we'll do a pilot.' Basically, that was pretty much it. But there was this moment where we looked at her and she went 'Is it funny?', like 'I don't know' – which is interesting. I bet she'll deny that. I bet she'll say: 'As soon as I saw it I knew that it was going be good', but Liam actually said: 'Yes, it is funny', so if anybody finally got the pilot commissioned it was him, I would say.

'It's always different if you're trying to sell something and you remember the situation as being like: "Oh my God, is this going to happen or not?"' suggests Root, who does indeed remember being impressed by the highlight tape. 'It was only five minutes long but very funny and gave you a sense that there was this great character here.' She says 'the decision to actually do a pilot wasn't hard' despite the potential drabness of the subject matter.

> People have afterwards often said to me it was a risky decision but it wasn't a very risky decision because it wasn't very expensive and it was very funny. It was probably not inappropriate for that time – the BBC's always been an organisation with management-speak and that kind of stuff, so I think the flavour of the tape was definitely appealing to the people watching it. Also I'd done a piece of work for the BBC before I was channel controller about younger audiences and one of the statistics was how many people met their partners in offices – that the office was a kind of hotbed of potential drama and sex and stuff like that. So there was a definitely a sense that the office as a set-up was something that was full of potential.

It's worth noting that the stage of development just described would be revisited in the final episode of *Extras*, Gervais and Merchant's 2005 sitcom about Andy Millman (Gervais), a 'background artist' with aspirations to at least a speaking role. In its own way, this show too was about workplace anxieties and frustrations: 'Everyone gets wound up with people they're working in close proximity with,' Andy suggests. In the sixth episode, Andy and his useless agent Darren Lamb (Merchant) are invited to the BBC to discuss a sitcom script Andy has submitted. During the meeting with the 'Head of New Comedy' – in fact shot in Plowman's office, naturally stripped of the *Office*-related paraphernalia usually on display – Andy is asked where he sees the project and expresses some ideas strikingly similar to Gervais and Merchant's own:

18

The pitch meeting: Merchant and Gervais in *Extras*, episode six (with Guy Henry). The scene was shot in Jon Plowman's office

19

BBC2 I think is really good for comedy. I think if you come up with a new project on BBC1 you've got to really water it down, do you know what I mean? I don't want a laughter track . . . I don't want it to be a comedy aimed at people without a sense of humour, if you know what I mean. I want people to be able to think about it. I don't want it filmed in front of a live studio audience. . . . I'd like to write it myself just because it's based on my own experiences, really. The character is based on a boss I used to work for and I just generally think the best things are auteured.

Andy also insists on playing the lead role himself (despite being, in Darren's words, 'a bit of a nobody') and stresses that 'I'm not sure about catchphrases . . . I just think catchphrases are too easy . . . they can get a little bit annoying after a while.' His script is redrafted with a producer and production of a pilot is approved.

Production

With a pilot episode commissioned and budgeted at £90,000, Merchant and Gervais were also determined to fix as many details as possible – a reaction to the troubled experience of shooting 'Golden Years' for Channel 4's *Comedy Lab*. Production restrictions had resulted in a sometimes frictive shoot, with the pair unpleasantly shocked by the lack of control they were ultimately able to exert over the realisation of their script. 'Because *Comedy Labs* are shot on such a shoestring budget, they didn't have the time or money to indulge us, so corners were cut, which we found frustrating,' Gervais recalls.

> We thought that our ace in the hole was that I was going to be in it, so at least we were going to be there anyway. You get horror stories of people sweating for three years over a script, handing it over, sitting down to watch it on telly and crying. And we thought that's it'd be okay because we'd be around, and that was enough for us. Then we realised it wasn't enough for us.

So when *The Office* got the go-ahead for a pilot, they decided 'we've got to direct this. It wasn't that we thought we were the best directors in the world, but we knew what we wanted to see on the telly.' Merchant adds,

> Our model was more those American sitcoms where the creators of the show are also the producers. And when they say 'producer' they really mean executive producer, overseer of it. So it's not that everyone else wasn't making their contribution, it's just that we weren't following the traditional formula of British television where you write something, it gets handed to a director and you step back. That wasn't the process with us. We went into a meeting and said: 'We want to write this and Ricky's going to be in it and we don't want any interference and we'd

like to direct it.' And they basically laughed at us and said: 'Who do you think you are?'

'That was something that took us all by surprise at the time,' Atalla confirms.

It was never discussed and I think we got the commission and then Ricky and Stephen said: 'We'd like to direct it,' and I was like: 'What? Would you? Really?' Because the conventional wisdom would be to get a director who's done it before.

Gupta recalls Plowman's hesitation at the idea. 'Jon was saying: "Not really very keen on that idea, given that you've never directed anything before." ' Again, the taster tape worked in the writers' favour, demonstrating their basic ability with a camera; but again it was not in itself sufficient to secure what they wanted. 'Stephen was clearly brilliant,' Plowman maintains, 'but he was inexperienced and it can just be that people, hard as they may work, find it quite a big overwhelming experience running a big crew.' 'So then there was a bit of an impasse reached at that point,' says Gupta. 'It looked like it was going to be a bit of a deal-breaker for them. They were quite adamant in how much control they wanted to retain.' Eventually a compromise solution was found, by which Gupta would take responsibility for directing the pilot but in practice it would be a collaborative effort with Merchant and Gervais. 'The understanding [with Ricky and Stephen] was always: "If that works and we go to a series, we'll sort of switch roles and you can take the helm directing but I'll be there in the background",' Gupta explains. 'So they were comfortable with that. I went to see Jon and he was comfortable with that, and so that's how we decided to progress from there.' 'I think that was only their natural hesitation,' Merchant now grants. 'Before you give people considerable sums of money you want to test the water.'

Preparations got underway, although shooting was not to start for some months. As well as the need to negotiate the BBC's funding

21

bureaucracy and Merchant and Gervais' other commitments, the writers were determinedly perfectionist. 'We did spend an awful lot of time on the script and casting because that's all we had,' Gervais recalls. 'That was our creation.' The process eventually paid off. Lucy Davis was cast relatively early as Dawn, having appeared in the BBC's *Pride and Prejudice* (1995) and *The Archers*. For the cynical, faintly desperate Tim they found Martin Freeman, who had appeared in some experimental BBC comedy including *Bruiser* (2000), to which Gervais had contributed material. For the other lead role, jobsworth and military fantasist Gareth, casting proved more challenging. Mackenzie Crook's scrawny frame, delicate features and translucent complexion were nothing like the thick-set squaddie type the writers had in mind for the character, but his approach – including the use of a West Country accent apparently suggested by Gervais (from Reading) and Merchant (from Bristol) – convinced them to revise their conception of the role. Gervais has said,

> What was exciting about Mackenzie is because he looks very fragile and vulnerable, not like we first imagined, we found that we could give him more and more ridiculous and horrendous lines and you still didn't mind because of his little bird-type face – like a little fledgling pigeon who hatched too early.[6]

'What linked all their performances was a great naturalism,' Atalla observes, 'just an easy way so that you couldn't see the acting cogs turning in their eyes.' Naturalism was also key to the location work – an unusual requirement for a situation comedy largely located in a single interior setting. Production manager Judith Bantock had recently finished a shoot at the Teddington Studios and suggested checking out the location – not the studio space, but some disused administrative facilities on the production site. Atalla recalls,

> They had some crappy old office space that needed retiling and I said: 'This could be perfect for us – this *is* a run-down office, you know? We

don't want to build flashy walls and flashy lights, we'll just put in a few partitions and more desks and this will be *The Office*'s office. Brent can sit in there.' We took the director of photography, Andy Hollis, round and said: 'Look, just make it look as crappy as it really does look. Let's not hide that stain in the carpet, let's not hide the marks that the dartboard has made on that bit of wall. Let's celebrate those coffee stains!'

Both script and production aspired to an unusually high level of naturalistic credibility. For Merchant,

The biggest governing thing was we wanted to make this as real as possible. We were obsessed with realism. Nothing could feel phoney. And so by having that as the guiding rule at least there's a coherence to it all: we can't have Dawn fall over because it's just too big a thing. It would be mad, you'd never see it in a real office.

23

'I think the realer you are the more you connect on an emotional level,' Gervais adds. This, he continues, also applied to narrative development.

We didn't want to cheat, we didn't want to use exposition. I never liked it when you get away with it in normal narrative dramas, when they'd walk in and say: 'John, you know your sister, the one that went to Guyana . . .?' But now we couldn't even expose plot because [the characters] were being filmed [and were therefore self-conscious]. The payback was this camera, bringing the public into it, so that became a bit of a godsend, that weighed it up a little bit, the fact that talking heads could explain things, could tell you about the character without huge scenes.

The area in which this obsession with realism was most evident was in the shooting style. Gervais says:

> We used to hate it when we'd see other fake documentaries – or rather
> spoof documentaries – where the camera crew were getting caught out
> or they were followed into a cupboard where they were shagging or
> taking a line of coke, or the boom was always in. Documentary teams
> don't do that. They make sure the boom's out, they clear up the
> [sensitive] stuff. So we cheated less than some real documentaries in a
> way, because we didn't want anyone to go: 'That wouldn't happen' or
> 'Why is there a film crew there?'

This insistence on shooting as if the action were unfolding unscripted in
front of a documentary crew meant, for instance, that close-ups and
reverse-angle shots (showing the same conversation from two different
perspectives) were largely prohibited, as a real-life crew would be
unable to get such footage without prior knowledge of the action or
restaging it. The realism of the set-up aided this fastidiousness, as
Gervais recalls:

24

> Because we didn't care for shooting from behind flames or lighting
> everything for three hours, we had fifteen takes at everything and that
> really came in useful because we'd get every little nuance. It didn't
> feel like the quest for perfection, it was: 'That's not what I was
> imagining.'

Such discipline had its drawbacks though, as Gervais would find out
during production of the series proper:

> I remember one scene I'd been looking forward to shooting for two
> months. I thought this was going to be the funniest thing ever, the
> scene where Brent reads Dawn a poem [in episode II.ii]. But it didn't
> quite work because they couldn't get in there; he'd never have allowed
> himself to break down or admit depression in front of the camera so it
> had to be spied on and that meant they couldn't get in close. We were

Pilot

really proud of sticking to our guns but it meant it wasn't as funny as it should have been.

As official director, Gupta was not always convinced of the benefits of such an approach.

There was lots of angsty hand-wringing about how authentic or not it was. You want to get it right but with hindsight, what a fucking waste of time a lot of it was. Who cares in the end? The style, the documentary feel, the wobbly whiz-pan – all of that is absolutely right. People know. I was always arguing you don't need to spell it out for them – seen enough of it, got it.

Atalla also felt that there may have been a disproportionate emphasis on perfecting the style.

I think I felt more than them that, rather than people loving it for a documentary, people would love it for the characters and the jokes, and that the documentary aspect of it was probably more in our minds as people who work in TV than it would be in the eyes of the viewer.

For Gervais and Merchant, however, this aspect was crucial.

I remember them worrying that we were obsessing about the documentary style but I don't think they appreciated how important the fake documentary style was. It was fundamental to how we were delivering these characters to the audience. The characters were funny and interesting because they were being filmed by a documentary team. After the TAPS taster, we realised that everything stemmed from how the characters' behaviour altered when the docu cameras were turning. The jokes were in the spaces between how they thought they were coming across and how the audience actually saw them. That's why we had to constantly stress the documentary team's presence. If the audience isn't constantly aware that they're watching a documentary, then they are just watching boring people in a boring office.

As shooting progressed, Merchant and Gervais assumed an increasing amount of directorial authority. 'We just thought: "There's no point to this",' the latter says. 'All we wanted to do was cut out the middle man, all we wanted to do was take out us having to put our hands up.' This shift was not, in principle, a hard one for Plowman to accept.

They were so passionate that they were going to do it and they were going to do it in their way and this was what it was going to be that in a way it's a no-brainer to say: 'All right, well, do it.' Because if you've got that much passion about doing it you don't need somebody else getting in the way of your vision. And if your vision's wrong then it'll just collapse and we won't do it [as a series].

There was still a certain amount of wrangling in post-production, with the producers keen to increase the pace of the action, but soon enough they came up with a satisfactory cut, including a tongue-in-cheek voice-over by John Nettles, narrator of the top-rated BBC1 docusoap, *Airport* (1996–). Gupta remembers 'sitting in Jon's office with Jon and Paul Jackson and Paul was very enthusiastic. But they weren't jumping up and down saying: "Oh my God, this is the greatest sitcom ever made in the UK." '

'I think it was liked,' Atalla concurs, 'but it was one of a number of shows at the same stage of that process. We were then one of fifteen fish swimming towards three holes, something like that.' As a cod documentary, *The Office* was hardly breaking new ground in BBC2 comedy: spoof observational documentary series *People Like Us* (BBC2, 1999) and *Operation Good Guys* (BBC2, 1997), the docusoap-style comedy about a bumbling police unit, were established successes. 'BBC2 has room for, say, three or four new comedies in a year,' Plowman explains, 'so if you're already doing something that's in a particular territory, you don't particularly want to compromise its success by doing another one.' Whether or not *The Office* would ever actually make it to broadcast was now in Jane Root's hands.

'I remember there was a big argument about should we do more *People Like Us* or should we do *The Office*,' Root recalls.

The worry was that we already had *People Like Us* and *Operation Good Guys*, and you wouldn't have wanted a schedule where you had *People Like Us* on at 9 o'clock and then *The Office* on at 9.30 and then *Good Guys* on at 10 o'clock. You had to balance it out.

By Root's reckoning, '*Good Guys* had pretty much run its course,' but *People Like Us* – the protracted production of the second series of which was already underway – presented more of a challenge. Gupta and Atalla were also aware that Plowman had been more closely involved in its development than he had been in *The Office*'s. Plowman grants,

> You're balancing things that are coming back that have been successful, but it's also about whether it feels new and adventurous and exciting, which *The Office* did. But how much would an audience enjoy being hoaxed, if you like? How much would they recognise that this was a comedy? Ricky's character is vulnerable but he's also dislikeable – you also go: 'Shut up, you're a prat. Stop being a prat.' And I think Jane particularly felt it was risky because there was nobody known in it.

Although as a creative gamble the stakes were quite high, in financial and logistical terms they were conspicuously low – an attribute that certainly counted in *The Office*'s favour. 'Oh, definitely,' Root confirms. 'Always does. At BBC2, you haven't got any money so something that looks like it could be great and not cost a fortune [is always welcome].' Ultimately the balance shifted in *The Office*'s favour and the commission was secured. 'I was a real fan of *People Like Us* but it had had two series by that point and it was hard to see where it'd go forward,' Root recalls. 'A kind of classic channel controller's decision.' It had been a close-run thing, a case of weighing up difficult options rather than waving it through – 'a sort of cautious commission, I think would be the best way of putting it,' Plowman suggests – but *The Office* was now confirmed to go into production as a six-part series for BBC2's 2001 schedule.

So Gervais and Merchant went off to write six half-hour scripts. Already they had a fairly advanced conception of the sweep of the story they wanted to tell, if not its detail. But, as Merchant explains, they had concerns that the pilot had become too conventional. 'We'd somehow written a sitcom rather than whatever we'd started with, this cobbled-together documentary. It was too structured, it had too much ebb and flow, it had too much of an arc, this kind of callback on previous jokes.' Gervais was concerned that

> It looked too interesting a place to work. We wanted to try and catch the existential futility of life and when people are too busy it looks like *Wall Street*. We wanted people looking bored. We wanted these people to wish they had something to do, so we [restored] that slowness that we had in the original [taster tape].

The documentary naturalism they were pursuing proved a valuable structuring tool. 'It made us more scrupulous in the writing process,' Merchant maintains.

> We'd sort of given ourselves this rod for our own back. If you're creating this hyper-real sensibility, suddenly anything phoney or plotty or sitcommy stands out. So that becomes troublesome because you've got to be constantly trying to disguise the coincidences, the convenience of people walking in and doing something, which you have to have for the comedy to be there.

In having to conceal the plot, Gervais notes, they were essentially doing the opposite of real-life docusoap-makers of the 1990s.

> They got everything and then tried to build a narrative around it, whatever way possible. They'd eke out something. So, with the joy that it's totally made up and we can have anything we wanted, we then had to go: 'But we've got to hide it because it's too good to be true.' We didn't have big plots anyway; we didn't have long lost brothers or it's built on an ancient burial ground or recreating a dinosaur. You know,

29

you work in an office and things like that don't happen. I've been in an office, about thirty people there. There was a screech of tyres – twenty people at the window. That's an incident! That's an event!

Although Gervais's recollection is that 'we didn't have a script editor', the show's producers remember reasonably substantial input. Gupta recalls,

The scripts would come in and they'd have lots of good jokes, but then you'd have to go: 'Okay, now we've got to make this something that works in terms of storytelling and structure.' And they worked hard at it, they put in the hours and they obviously knew what they were doing.

Gupta also remembers having to rein in some of the more provocative material in keeping with Gervais' earlier work.

Ricky loves that: 'How far can I go to really appal people? Oh, I'll do some jokes about race, then I'll do some jokes about disability, then I'll do some jokes about ethnic minorities with disabilities and gender issues.' He'll just keep pushing it and you'll go: 'Yeah, don't know about that one, you may have crossed the line there.'

The show's conspicuous banality and frequent embarrassment also proved challenging, Gupta admits.

I kept saying: 'Don't push too far because you don't want to alienate people,' and Ricky was like: 'I don't care if only ten people watch the show as long as they're the right ten people.' And I was like: 'That's the biggest pile of crap I've ever heard. If you only want ten people to watch your show go and do it in a pub in Islington.'

Atalla had similar reservations.

> I always wanted a little bit more action in those early days because I was worried that we would lose our audience, or not even get them in the first place. There was a moment in the first episode when Gareth's stapler gets put into some jelly – by the standards of *The Office* it was a big set-piece gag, and those sort of moments happened less and less, but at the beginning it was important for those bits to be there, because they're the bits that people like. I was worried that there weren't enough of those. You have to earn the right to have long pauses or silence in comedy – people have to be bothered to sit down and watch it in a world of tons of choice.

As the shoot approached, the formal approach was also tweaked. In emulating documentary procedure so closely, the pilot had contained many long takes in medium shot but no close-ups beyond the talking heads; this, combined with the understated performances and the extra filter of the voice-over, resulted in a somewhat cool effect. 'The way it was filmed made it harder to love the show,' Atalla suggests.

31

> It was obvious watching that pilot back that if you stripped off that voice-over and just told the story, it would probably be stronger for it – that the best bits of the show were just the actors at work, and the commentary felt forced.

Merchant agrees that 'it worked against that suspension of disbelief if a voice constantly snapped you out of it.' The move away from genre pastiche had its losses too, Gervais says.

> There was one scene in the pilot where we pixellated out someone's face, like they didn't want to be part of it. And I was crying with

laughter. But it was too clever, too postmodern – we didn't want people to even think about the mechanics of making the programme because we wanted them to watch it like they watch a drama or a sitcom.

Merchant and Gervais were confirmed as directors for the series proper ('I never had a problem with that,' Root says, 'because again it was fairly low cost'), their inexperience offset by bullish self-belief and the words of those they admired. 'All we knew was that our favourite projects over the past fifty years have been auteured,' Gervais says.

We were fans of everyone from Billy Wilder to Woody Allen. We almost learned things academically up until the point of experience. Like that brilliant Billy Wilder quote, the ten commandments – the first nine are 'thou shalt not bore' and the tenth one is 'get final edit'.

Merchant confirms that it was 'all just reading things like Kubrick – "Ninety per cent of the work is casting." Arbitrary things you'd read and go: "Well, that sounds right." '

Merchant remembers 'Ricky suggested a rule, which we stuck to, which was we don't put anything in unless you both agree that it's right.' Gervais stresses this approach was a mutual safety net to protect both men's extremely high expectations.

We didn't necessarily think that was the best way to make the programme, but it was so much more important to both of us not to put something that we didn't want in than to cut something that we did want in. We just didn't want that thing to be compromised at all. And now I know that when we look at it we might see things and think: 'Oh, we could have done that better,' but we'll never go: 'Fucking hell, I told you that was fucking wrong.' It's very strange, it was almost like we knew that the legacy was more important than the moment. We said: 'We want something on our shelves that we're proud of.'

Merchant concurs: 'All I ever wanted was something I could put on my shelf, so that I could say: "Yeah, I made that." '

The pair's expectations and nerves at taking on sole responsibility were evident to Gupta too.

Once we started doing the series and they were doing the directing, there was more tension because they were so nervous, so uptight. It was a big thing for them. They knew this was their big shot and they didn't want to fuck it up.

Gervais recalls his trepidation.

I remember I panicked about a week before we first started shooting. I came to Steve and I said: 'I'm really worried that this is the sitcom that we said we wouldn't do.' In our minds it was too slick. I remember feeling that we were worried about putting in the scene where I go: 'I think I've found a lump,' and that to me sums up *The Office* – that strange, oppressive thing of someone sitting alone reading and the boss coming up and going: 'Had a bit of a scare, found a lump.' And I thought: 'That's what's not on telly.' We weren't trying to be too innovative but what we didn't want to do was just churn out another sitcom.

Once the shoot actually got underway in January 2001, this combination of cockiness, ambition and inexperience was not always easy to work with.'Ricky and Steve's default position was: "Nobody apart from us knows what they're talking about",' Gupta recalls. 'It was slightly prickly, because while they knew what they wanted, they didn't know how to go about it necessarily.' 'We were confident, we weren't arrogant,' Merchant maintains. 'We put our hand up straight away and said: "Look, we don't really know what we're doing," and so we were always asking everyone else's opinion.' Still, he admits to an element of over-confidence.

> We thought it would be easier than it was. We thought that because it was like a documentary that would make it really easy, you wouldn't have to know everything about lenses and tracking. It never occurred to us that it was an ambitious project, we always thought it was such a lo-fi thing. We thought: 'How can we go wrong? It's so simple.' You'd go on location and it was like: 'Why do all these people need to come? Just bring the camera.'

The most obvious symptom of this inexperience was a massively inflated shooting ratio – that is, they were recording far more material than could ever be used. 'We were probably shooting too much to begin with,' Merchant says. 'We were panicked that we wouldn't have enough coverage so we were shooting everything from every angle with every size of frame. It was getting a bit mad.' Gupta remembers that

> After the first couple of days, the production manager came in and said: 'Look, your shooting ratio is a problem – it's like forty-eight to one or something.' We did have to say: 'You've really got to think a bit more clearly about this. We can't just shoot.' And they were going: 'Well, why not? Why not?' And I was saying: 'Well, it's going to take you forever to edit it – just watching all the different takes will take you two years.'

So each evening Gupta would join Gervais and Merchant in the pub and – 'knowing they were under pressure and they were slightly spiky characters' – try to suggest alternative planning strategies to minimise on-set experimentation.

34

Luckily, the circumstances of the shoot were relatively forgiving. 'Because we were in one place with one camera with no lighting issues, it was all acting,' Gervais says. Gupta concedes that

> We had the luxury of fannying about a bit. You weren't like: 'We've got an hour to get this shot in this location and then we've got to go halfway across London.' If it had been one of those shows, we'd have been royally screwed because they'd never have been able to shoot it. It would have got ugly – someone would have come and said: 'Right, I'm taking over.'

Plowman thinks

> It was nervousness, and partly because Ricky was directing it with Stephen and so he would do a take and then he'd go out and have a look at it and think: 'I can do that better'. But I do remember thinking: 'Oh God, am I going to have to go in and get heavy with them?' or 'Am I going to have to change the director?' or 'Is this really going to cost a fortune because they're shooting so much?'

Nerves subsided after a week or two, as the quality of the work became clear, Atalla recalls. 'Ricky and Stephen got more and more adept and learned very quickly.' Their almost zealous determination to play by the rules remained, however. 'If you know the truth, you can't get it wrong,' Gervais maintains. 'It's only if you haven't really decided that you get inconsistencies.' This approach went so far as to imagine those doing the 'filming' within the fictional situation. 'You end up making the invisible documentary team, you're sort of aware of them in a sense,' says Merchant.

> Even though you haven't given them names and you don't know how many there are, they're another character almost in the show and so

you have to think them through as rigorously as you would anything else. So we would almost decide: 'Well, is there two camera crews now, have they brought in a second camera for today? Where is this person?'

The scripts were largely followed with a similar rigour. 'We'd been through a lot of improvisation in terms of arguing between Tim and Gareth and things like that that we didn't really use,' Merchant says. 'It was like: "We spent a year working on this. By all means, we're open to suggestion, but let's not pretend that it's a free-for-all." ' 'I'm not open to suggestion,' Gervais chips in. 'It annoyed me. Ad libs make the crew laugh more 'cause they haven't heard them, but when you get back into the edit, the written lines are better.' An exception was Tim and Dawn's flirting. 'We tried writing it but it sounded too written,' Merchant says, 'so we'd give them a topic to talk about and then they might give ten minutes and we'd lift a little bit.' (Davis exploited the situation much as some of the characters themselves would: in real life she likes having her hair played with 'so I thought: "Oh, I'll incorporate that, 'cause he can't say no, we're on camera." '[7])

Gervais was just as inexperienced in performance as in directing and was, Gupta recalls, ignorant of 'things that actors are taught about film-making, like not to talk when the other guy's talking because it'll make the editing difficult.' 'I don't know what I'm doing,' Gervais admits.

> Little things like hitting your mark, which I just ignored in the first series. I really didn't want to look like I was acting. It's just by the second series I'd sort of learned that I could still give that but I could stand on a mark and walk into a room, 'cause I was just more confident as an actor.

Equally disruptive was his tendency to prompt other performers into corpsing with ad libs. 'He's not the most generous actor in the world,' Gupta says.

36

He gets very bored very easily so once he's done his bit, the rest is a bit boring now. 'Boring, boring! We're on your shot, I will amuse myself by pissing about and trying to make you laugh and doing anything other than actually helping you in your work.'

Gervais was prone too to cracking up on his own lines, though, as Merchant reminds him, 'When someone says: "Five minutes until lunch," you suddenly snap into action. It's amazing how quickly then you can remember your lines.'

'My biggest learning curve was once we started editing,' Merchant says.

For instance, we shot a lot of documentary-style GVs – general views – of specific stuff, like you'd see in a documentary: close-ups of stuff on people's desks or hands typing. And we tried to put it in but the

General view of not a lot

problem was it makes it look too busy, too interesting. The only stuff we used of the GVs were these big wide empty shots with nothing going on. So then for the second series we scrapped all the other type of GVs and we only ever shot those big wide shots. We discovered that aspect in the editing of the first series and it meant that we could expand it and apply it more in the second series.

There was still, Merchant recalls, a scare to come. 'We got a little bit pissed one evening and watched a rough cut that someone had sent us. We hadn't seen anything, and we got really depressed.' 'I nearly cried,' Gervais says.

We were going: 'We've fucked this. What the fuck have we done? This is awful, this is rubbish.' And then we went and had a chat with the editor and said: 'Look, we've just got to reassure ourselves.' We played around a little bit and we realised it was all because he was editing it like a traditional sitcom – and to be fair to him he'd had no reason not to. So once we started re-editing it we realised that we were okay.

A theme tune was also required. 'There was a Cat Stevens song originally that we were looking at,' Atalla remembers.[8]

'Handbags and Gladrags' was something Ricky and Stephen chose. I couldn't persuade Rod Stewart's people to let us use their version [the well-known 1970 cover] so we got permission to rerecord it. We did that in a little studio in Camden with Big George [Webley], who composed the theme tune to *Have I Got News for You* [1990–]; he assembled a very good session band and a guy called Fin sang the vocal. And then of course [after the series went out] the Stereophonics released their version and that kind of helped as well – suddenly the theme tune associated with us was at number two in the charts. I remember getting a call from their people asking would we use their version on the second series and it was like: 'Well, why would we now change our version? What would be in it for us?'

The series was duly delivered to BBC2. 'Once it turned up we all thought it was great,' recalls Root. 'The tough thing then was how to get people to find it – often on BBC2 you can end up with great sitcoms that people don't discover.' Transmission of the first episode was scheduled for 9 July 2001 – not a conventionally prestigious slot like the autumn or New Year schedules. Plowman describes it as 'a cautious transmission, very quiet, very unpublicised, and in a way it was absolutely the best thing that could have happened to it'. Root agrees:

> There's always been a historical sense that people don't want new shows starting in summer because there's this completely wrong idea that everyone is on holiday. But it does mean that there's fewer big ITV and BBC1 shows being launched and you can often get more press and get more talked about than if you're launched against big things. And I think there were some very good trails. And so we just kind of sat and waited then, which is what you have to do.

Broadcast and beyond

Early ratings were disappointing. Atalla remembers

> being at my sister's graduation the morning after our first ever show and someone called me up from the BBC and said: 'You got 1.4 million.' I remember being disappointed and anxious about those figures. You're not far from hanging by a string at that point.

In addition to attracting so few viewers, the show also scored badly on the audience appreciation index ('AIs'), data gathered to assess how much those who did watch the show actually enjoyed it. Only one other new addition to BBC2's line-up scored lower in that year's AIs: women's bowls. 'The first figures were really terrible,' Root confirms.

> We didn't understand it, we really didn't. The fact that the AIs were so low made me think that there was something going on there that people just didn't understand. I remember there was a meeting we had: 'Oh God, how are we going to get people to like this?' It took a while for people to catch on.

Gupta recalls that 'anecdotally you hear a lot of people didn't get that it was comedy, they genuinely thought it was a docusoap or genuinely didn't understand that it was supposed to be funny.'

40

Some solace was offered by the near-universally warm critical reception from the *Guardian* (which welcomed the first episode as 'extremely promising') to the *Daily Mail* (which by the third found it 'truly magnificent . . . near-perfect') to the *People* ('a work of comic genius'). Plowman suggests that this might have been helped by the low-profile launch: 'The critics like it more because they feel they've discovered it.'

Ratings remained low, however. Gupta remembers seeing scheduler Liam Keelan. 'I bumped into Liam in the lift and said: "Hey, isn't it great? *The Office*, fantastic press." And he said: "Yeah, shame about the figures," and got out of the lift.' 'We got 1.4 million three weeks in a row,' Atalla recalls.

> I remember Ricky saying: 'What does that mean?' and I said: 'It means we don't really want to be going down from there, because if you start heading towards a million then you may not get recommissioned.' We certainly didn't have any downward manoeuvrability, to put it bluntly.

As Plowman explains,

> The ratings curve for a comedy on BBC1 is you get your highest
> audience on the first show, then it goes down and you know you've got
> a hit if gradually over the other four or five episodes it creeps up again.
> On BBC2 you want to be going up a hill – preferably up a steep hill but
> any hill is better than downhill or a straight road.

The show retained its critical success and word-of-mouth
currency, and Root also remembers increasing the number of trailers:
'The summer thing was important, that meant there was a
comparatively large amount of trails available, whereas if you put it in
the winter or at some other time when you're trying to launch a whole
load of other shows then it's much harder.' Eventually both AI ratings
and viewing figures increased. 'In week four we got 1.7 million,' says
Atalla, 'and I think then we got 1.9m and then 2.1m and then back to
1.9m for the last one.' This was the pattern they'd been hoping for, 'so it
was doing the right thing.' This proved enough to secure the commission
of a second series within a week of the last episode's transmission on 20
August. For Root

> That wasn't a difficult decision. It always makes for a better story if you
> can make it out to be a hellish decision where you had to fight to get
> these things made. Lots of other things I do remember huge battles
> about – whether one could afford it or whether one should do it or not –
> but this was not one of them.

Plowman too 'can't remember any question' about a recommission; for
Atalla, having achieved a boost in its final weeks, 'it never felt in the
balance that there would be a second series.'

There was further affirmation in the show's winning 'Best New
Comedy' at the British Comedy Awards that December. Judging that the
show's word-of-mouth appeal had not had time to be fully reflected in

41

the ratings, Root took the unusual decision to repeat the series within six months (in January 2002) in a better slot (at 10 pm, against the news on both BBC1 and ITV, rather than 9.30 pm). It paid off: *The Office* achieved the rare feat of increasing its ratings on a repeat run, averaging 2.3 million viewers compared to the first run's 1.6 million. 'All those people who were talking about catching it second time did catch it second time, and the press picked up on it a lot more,' notes Atalla, who also credits this increased exposure with the show's nomination in that year's BAFTAs, for Best Sitcom and Best Comedy Performance for Gervais – both of which they won that April.

Other awards followed too, which combined with the higher ratings and practical experience gained on the first series to make the writing and shooting of *The Office* series two relatively plain sailing. Where the first batch of scripts had required a degree of redrafting, Gervais' recollection is that those for series two (and, later, the Christmas Specials) were 'on the nail', aided by the ability to write for an established cast and play to their strengths. The general sense of assurance contrasted with the anxiety of the first shoot: 'I really felt then that I could say we were proper writer–directors,' says Gervais, 'and I started getting good at acting.' Atalla felt 'Ricky and Stephen had really grown in stature as directors, I think that was a key leap', and was significantly more confident himself: 'a bit of colour drove into your face, you know, that you had not sunk without trace. It was a case of struggling to get it right rather than worrying about the formula.' Gupta accordingly became a regular rather than daily presence on set.

There was still hesitation over certain scenes – often those that would become familiar as stand-out moments. David Brent's notorious dance for II.v – the incident that was to become emblematic of the show – was one of these. Gervais remembers:

> I was worried about the idea. There was one thing that I used to do to make Steve laugh, 80s dancing. He said it was so funny, a fat bloke trying to dance, so we decided to put that in. But then we went: 'Well,

we can't just put it in, it's not allowed.' We hated it when we saw things just pop up 'cause that was somebody's set-piece, so we had to work back: why would he do that? Well, maybe Neil, his nemesis, does a good one; maybe it's Red Nose Day, his favourite day . . . So suddenly, just to get to one little bit, we have this whole fucking iceberg under the water that we have to do just to justify that, so people didn't go: 'That's just Ricky's set-piece that he likes doing.' Which is true.

Merchant concurs:

We were worried that it would be out of place in the show . . . We never thought people would come up and do it in the street. It never occurred to us that it would become a sort of trademark of the show. I always think that it's a shame that it did, because I'm sure people watched the Christmas Specials expecting to see funny dances all the way through.

43

Merchant acknowledges that *The Office*

became perhaps more sitcommy in the second series. What you realise when you're writing is that you can't just repeat what you've already done, it has to move on, the jokes have to get slightly bigger because it's not enough any more for Brent to just quietly embarrass himself.

Conversely, there was some anxiety over whether the climactic moments of the series would place too great a demand on the audience's emotional engagement. The sequence in which Tim removes his microphone to make a second appeal to Dawn was, Atalla says, 'a pretty audacious manoeuvre. There'd be nothing worse than if you do that trick and as a viewer you're sitting there thinking: "I don't really give a fuck what they're saying anyway." ' It was a single shot that began as one of Tim's talking heads before breaching that particular form, the camera following him down the corridor when he suddenly decides to act on his feelings.

> I remember doing a lot of takes of that, trying to get the run of Tim chasing Dawn up and that feeling that the camera was just behind and trying to catch up with them, and that Tim wanted to say something to her but was aware that he had said stuff before that had been broadcast and had embarrassed him. We were all worried but the silence ended up being very powerful. Ricky and Stephen were very adamant about that. What was good about it was that it wasn't like a sudden break of the rules that we'd worked so hard to make for the show – it was fitted perfectly within them but it was a different thing to observe.

The other, equally emotive climax of II.vi was Brent's tearful begging to keep his job. Gervais admits,

> This'll sound ridiculous and pretentious, but the bit where I cry at the end, we wanted Brent to be really cocky so you didn't see it coming, and the influence for that was *Angels with Dirty Faces*, where he's going: 'I'm going to sit down and take it like a short back and sides and spit in his face'[9] and then he cries, and you don't see it coming. Totally different, but it's the fact that he thinks: 'Of course, yeah, I know what I've got to do, I've got to be really cocky like I don't care.'

As they had occasionally done elsewhere, Gervais and Merchant broke their own rules for the scene, using a two-camera set-up 'because I actually thought I could only do it once and we wanted the real reactions of Stirling [Gallacher] and Patrick [Baladi]. I just wanted to cry and see what they did.' Gupta recalls

It was the first scene of the day and Ricky came in and he was quite jumpy. The second series was really relaxed – the show had done well, everyone was happy, it was all jolly – but that day he was quite jumpy because obviously it was going to be this big scene and I thought: 'Well, he's not an actor, I don't know how he's going do this.' And he came out on the first take, did it, and it was electric. Everyone was dead quiet and it was all like: 'Oh, my God' and Lucy [Cain] the make-up lady was crying. It was like: 'I didn't know he could do that, that's extraordinary.' Because suddenly you realised Brent was a human being: he's not some monster, he's maybe a bit misguided but he's a person; of course you feel for him. Most people watched that and thought: 'Oh my God, poor guy.'

Where the first series had initially struggled to get noticed, the second was greeted with considerable anticipation in both broadsheets and tabloids: the *Mirror* invented a quiz to help readers identify which character they most closely resembled while the *Daily Star* ran a guide to 'Who's Who in *The Office*' on the day of the first episode, 30 September 2002. With a peak audience of 5.2 million, II.i gained the largest audience of any *Office* episode until the Christmas Specials; expectation was such that most critics opened their reviews by wondering whether a new series could stand up to the first (and concluding that it could). The figures did not, however, stay high: by the end of II.i the audience had dropped below 4.8 million and continued to fall. Viewing figures for II.ii averaged 3.6 million and had dropped to 3.4 million by II.iv, before climbing again to close at 4.4 million for the last episode. This might suggest that general audiences in fact found the series harder going than the media professionals who consistently championed it; even so, its ratings and audience share remained considerably higher than BBC2's average, and it was unbeaten in its slot for at least the first four weeks of its run. The DVD of the first series – released midway through transmission of the second – became the BBC's fastest-selling TV series, selling 80,000 copies in its first week. Coverage remained extensive throughout, with the *Express* even running a piece containing legal advice to Brent after his arguably unfair dismissal. (The character was indeed revealed in the Christmas Specials to have won a tribunal.)

The second series certainly cemented the show's place in mainstream culture. Atalla began noticing that 'the *Sun* would slap a big picture of David Brent over any boss who was caught doing anything bad in the workplace', awards kept coming (Gervais beat Freeman to win Best Comedy Actor at that year's British Comedy Awards) and by Christmas over a million copies of the first series had been sold (of which over 683,000 were on DVD, making it the format's biggest-selling TV title to date). Jane Root publicly made *The Office*'s return her New Year's resolution for 2003. 'I really hoped that there would be more,' she says. 'I'd be lying if I said otherwise. It's a channel controller's job to try and get more of things like that, and equally it's up to Ricky and Stephen to manage their own creativity and their own careers.' Atalla was also keen for a third series – 'it's not a case of milking it, it's just a case of making sure that it's had its proper life' – but Gervais and Merchant doubted the programme could sustain a further six-episode series. 'It got to the point where the most famous thing was the dance, which in our minds was never typical of the show,' says Merchant. 'I don't know how we could have carried on going without it starting to refer back to itself and have people expecting big comedy set-pieces. You'd have had to trowel it on.'

As they had not yet finished telling the story they had set out to tell, however, the writers eventually decided to revive *The Office* as a two-part special, to be broadcast the following Christmas. The resolution of Tim and Dawn's slow-burning romance was the main impetus. 'We always intended to get them together,' Gervais insists.

> That wasn't an afterthought, we didn't start thinking about that on November 3rd: 'Tell you what, as it's Christmas, let's get them together.' We knew the trajectory as we were writing it – that was the beauty of knowing it was a finite thing, we knew where we wanted to end up.

Writing proceeded with the usual perfectionism, especially regarding Dawn and Lee's status as unofficial long-term residents in Florida. 'We phoned the American embassy to find out how long someone could be there, why could they be there, could they work,' Gervais recalls. 'We got so much information I was wondering if he thought I wanted to become an illegal alien.' The location for the scenes set in Florida also had to ring true. In the event the summer of 2003 saw a record-breaking heatwave but, as Atalla explains,

> You have to make that call quite early. There are parts of Devon where you can apparently get a place that looks like Florida but I said: 'What are we going to do if it's an English summer? It'll be the first bit of the show that looks like we've cheated.' Florida's a long way to go and they're small scenes, so in the end we combined it with a shorter trip to Spain.

Merchant and Gervais had realised that having sent Dawn and Lee to the US at the end of the second series, they had to come up with a plausible reason for both a camera crew's presence in Florida and their return to the UK. Here, however, the documentary format offered its own *deus ex machina* solution. 'We just thought: "Well, look, documentary teams interfere," ' says Gervais. Merchant continues:

> If they have the same emotions as the audience, they want to reunite those two people because they know it will be both dramatically interesting and good television. So it would be in the interests of the documentary team to get those people back. It would be legitimate.

'We did everything out in the open,' Gervais insists. 'You hear [the director] say: "Do you want to go back?" They can't have us on it.'

As usual, the imaginary crew within the series was fully conceived – 'we decided there were three camera teams individually trailing Brent, Tim and Dawn,' Merchant recalls – but for the first time they were evident to the audience, through off-screen questions. There were also captions and other tropes that made the presence of a crew more explicit. It was considered important to stress this aspect, Gervais says, because

> if it was a real documentary, they'd be famous – it would have gone out on television. So those people now have to acknowledge the fact that they were on telly and they saw the documentary, and so did the rest of the world.

They also wanted to remind the audience of this dynamic, says Merchant:

> We were worried that by the end of the second series people had got used to the fake documentary aspect and perhaps they weren't really watching it with that in mind any more, they were watching it like a regular sitcom.

The other major change was the announcement in August 2003 that the Christmas Specials would screen on BBC1 – a sure sign of the Corporation's belief that the show had the potential to attract a significantly higher audience than even the second series had gained. *The Office*'s established appeal was confirmed when the second series sold over 143,000 DVDs on its release in October 2003, replacing the first series as Britain's fastest-selling TV release. Plowman suggests that

> the scramble to get the Christmas Specials on BBC1 may tell you something about the way television's developed in the past ten years – the way in which you go: 'That's a hit, I want it now!' if you're a Controller. It also tells you that comedies are something the BBC does

and nobody else does as much, so if you've got a comedy you want to kind of wave it around.

It was perhaps apt that a show about the vagaries of the workplace provoked some contentious office politics within the BBC. Atalla remembers that

The politics of that were bad actually, were difficult. Jane Root was very sore about losing it. It was a show that was very associated with BBC2 and we were caught between being loyal to Jane, who we all liked, and the inevitable point that we'd get more viewers on BBC1. My point to Ricky and Stephen was that were it any other time of year it wouldn't justify the move, but BBC1 and ITV are the channels of Christmas Day and the day after – you don't watch edgy BBC2 because your gran's there. So everyone's watching BBC1 and ITV and if we weren't on BBC1, BBC1 would put up something big against us. I felt bad for BBC2, and for Jane particularly because she'd grown the show on BBC2. And I'm not sure how well it was dealt with internally. I remember one very difficult meeting with Jane.

Root admits to it being – to say the least – a bittersweet turn of events.

It was. It's the moment in every BBC2 controller's life where you've created this great thing and suddenly it disappears. You have to try and wish it well but it's upsetting, especially as by that point we knew it wasn't coming back [for any more shows]; it wasn't a matter of something moving that we felt was going to have a much longer life on BBC1.

Still, Atalla recalls that Root 'was very gracious about it in the end, and she said those last two absolutely looked and felt right on BBC1, like its proper place'. Root observes that

49

In the end it's fantastically romantic – love triumphs. I think that's the big thing that I'd say about *The Office*, that it does have warmth and affection at its heart. There's quite a lot of BBC2 great comedy that's actually quite bitter and misanthropist: Alan Partridge is a brilliant comic creation but in the end Steve Coogan doesn't love Alan Partridge, he kind of hates him. Whereas there's an enormous amount of love and affection [in *The Office*], and I think that's why it became such a beloved thing. David Brent is a monster but he's also a monster that Ricky clearly cares about. That redeeming love of the characters – all of them, even the terrible ones – is, I think, the thing that made people much more affectionate towards it than one might have guessed.

Gupta agrees:

I think that's absolutely integral to how it ended up on BBC1 getting six or seven million viewers rather than staying on BBC2 and getting two million. You read stuff in papers saying: '*The Office* is the comedy of discomfort and it's all about being nasty.' No, it's not! Yes, it's uncomfortable because it's embarrassing, but actually the stories in *The Office* are about people and humanity. It's about unrequited love – what's horrible about that?

This was something BBC1 required a degree of reassurance over, Merchant recalls.

I think what worried them initially is that they thought we were going to be avant-garde or maverick, and I think what they discovered was that actually we're quite traditional, both in terms of our respect for the budget – we aren't wayward, we aren't coke addicts, we aren't Michael Cimino high on his own skill, we're a bit puritanical in many respects – and also that we actually were going to make it an upbeat ending, so it was going to be feel-good. It wasn't going to be this weird sort of leftfield Dennis Potter. It was always going to be pretty mainstream really, but on its own terms.

Gervais adds, 'it's only the sensibilities that weren't mainstream, the rendering of it: no laughter track, no unfeasibly clever handsome people cutting on one-liners and no convoluted plots. But the Christmas Special is the only time we even sewed up a bit of closure, and not too much; they didn't get married six months later, we only left them with a flavour.'

Despite the move, there was no attempt to soften the tone. 'We didn't water it down for BBC1,' Gervais insists. Merchant adds:

With the first half of the Christmas Special we tried to go right back to what we'd done originally – we tried to make it dark and slow-burning. We were worried that suddenly they were going to stick it on BBC1 and this was going to be a big Christmas romp, and we were like: 'Well, fuck that.' We also wanted the pay-off at the end to be all the more rich because it was miserable.

Shooting also went smoothly and without pressure from the Corporation. 'They didn't even know how long it was going to be until we handed it in, they were that flexible,' Gervais recalls.

As with the second series, transmission (on 26 and 27 December) was heavily anticipated in the press; the reviews were again ecstatic despite professed concerns that the Specials would disappoint in comparison to the series; there was particular praise for the show's delivering an upbeat ending without sentimentality or a change in tone. The ratings were also impressive: although not in the league of *Only Fools and Horses*, which had 16.4 million viewers on Christmas Day, *The Office* attracted a peak audience of 7.2 million – a thirty-one per cent share of the audience – for the first show, dropping to an average of

51

6.1 million for the second. 'I think the first episode alienated a lot of people,' Merchant suggests,

> particularly newcomers who only really knew of it from funny dances on clip shows. I was in the pub and I heard people slagging it off: 'I didn't think much of *The Office* last night, I switched it off after ten minutes.' And why not? It's BBC1, it's Christmas, why should they expect a fairly low-key, quite depressing [programme]?

Gervais suggests an alternative reading of the figures:

> I don't think it did get people dipping in it for it because even though our average [for the series] was five million, with the repeats and everything I bet we probably had ten million people that had ever watched it and quite liked it – they just didn't all watch it all at once. So I think [the audience for the Christmas Specials] probably was people that had seen it before.

After the success of the Specials, the idea of a further series was inevitably raised but this wasn't an option for the writers. 'We thought we might have blown it by doing the Christmas Special,' says Gervais. 'We could have packed it a little bit tighter and probably put it all in two series.' As Atalla notes, 'Nobody felt cheated at the end, nobody says *The Office* ended too early and really when you watched the second of the Christmas Specials you just thought: "That's that – that has finished." ' On a practical level, Merchant cites the risk of the writing process becoming repetitive – 'the conventions of sitcom are like: "God, what, do we have to do this for five or six years, like every year we do another series …?" ' – and Gervais describes the intensity of their involvement:

We write it, we direct it, we're in it, editing, worrying about the DVD. We worry about the font, we worry about where it's placed in the shot, we do our own publicity. It's a full time job. An actor can do six sitcoms a year, so can a director, so can a writer, but when you do it all you're in it for the long haul and it's exhausting, you know. We might as well have worked in the office in Slough for three years.

53

Welcome to Wernham Hogg

In the office, a well-fed, self-satisfied man in a scrubby goatee and his late thirties is reclining behind his desk, clicking a biro. 'I don't give shitty jobs,' he pronounces.

> If a good man [he points across the desk and the camera pulls back to reveal Alex, a young worker] comes to me and says: 'Thank you, David, for the opportunity and continued support in the work-related arena, but I've done that, I wanna better myself, I wanna move on,' then I can make that dream come true, too, aka for you.

With the confidence of a big fish in a small pond (the cheesy self-congratulatory grin, the gunslinger's toss of the phone from right hand to left), he places a call ('Sammy, you old slag!') and swings Alex a job as a forklift truck driver on the basis of credentials he falsifies on the spot, gleefully miming a Pinocchio nose and crossing himself as he does so. As a final confirmation of his alpha-male status, he facetiously asks whether Sammy's wife has left him yet. The conversation stalls and he hangs up. 'She has left him,' he gulps. 'I forgot about that.' His eyes swing round to meet the camera, trapped yet defiant, features fixed in a self-conscious grimace of mortification.

The opening scene of the first episode of *The Office* is a great introduction, and not only to the character of David Brent – the deluded attribution of words and sentiments to others, the hapless attempted

Smug/mortified: the opening scene of I.i

combination of chumminess and self-aggrandisement, the yearning for an appreciative supplicant audience, the final failure to meet even his own expectations – and his performance by Ricky Gervais: the runaway hand gestures, the smug self-congratulation, the panicked flash of self-doubt. The scene also neatly illustrates the sophisticated balancing act between registers that characterises the series as a whole. Brent's phone conversation is addressed to at least three audiences: to Sammy, he's discussing a new employee; to Alex, he's demonstrating his clout and magnanimity; and to the camera crew (and, through them, the audience at home), he's showing what a great boss-cum-entertainer he is. Time and again, the botched negotiation of such boundaries will be central to the series' action, and in Brent's case it's usually that desperate stare into the camera he's tried so hard to nonchalantly charm that gives the game away.

A similar range of addresses marks *The Office* out as unusual: superficially it has all too much in common with the tedious milieu it describes, conspicuously lacking conventional appeals to audience sympathy. Yet its very banality offers a more authentic view of the workplace than most TV series, showing an environment with which many viewers could all too easily associate. Once acclimatised to the series' pace and style, they could also identify the set-up's considerable comic value and, perhaps more surprisingly, its emotional substance too. Where many conventional sitcoms use mundane settings as the springboard for escapist fancy, *The Office* embraces mundanity as its main mode and subject. Indeed, this is crucial to the central irony of the character of David Brent: although he would like to believe that he has established an environment suffused with the heightened wackiness of a conventional sitcom, to his staff and the audience, Wernham Hogg remains achingly uninvigorating. By ordinary sitcom standards, very little happens in any given episode of *The Office* in terms of plot and action: the characters don't put elaborate schemes into effect and then struggle against their collapse; the underlying situation isn't challenged in the localised way sitcom often demands, from the unruly women of the Lucille Ball school to the bids for escape of the Trotters or Father Ted. In fact the *status quo* is under a profound existential threat: early in the first episode, the Slough branch of Wernham Hogg is threatened with closure, and the whole first series plays out against this backdrop of jeopardy. Yet the immediate responses to the threat of redundancy are universally blasé, and although concern mounts over the series, the comic effects are derived from Brent's disastrous negotiation of the situation rather than his employees' standing.

The setting too contains little to set the pulse racing. The opening title sequence is a perfect capsule of mundanity. Uninviting, uninvolving, uninspiring, it offers drumbeats, descending minor chords and five shades of grey; overcast skies, wet tarmac and monotonous traffic; cage-like building facades and a plughole of a roundabout. It isn't hard to see why some viewers initially hesitated to identify *The Office* as a comedy when its first impression is so unrelentingly drab. No jaunty, jangly theme tune here, no roll-call of characters laying out their shtick; no faces at all, in fact. The setting seems more geometric than human, moving from a composition of black-windowed blocks to the side of a bus – a sliver of drab, grubby yellow. In a long shot of a roundabout, traffic continues the bus's leftward trajectory before looping back round on itself, the promise of movement supplanted by a routine cycle. A sign locates us on the road to the Slough Trading Estate, its icon of an articulated lorry instantly illustrated by a real one heaving into shot, much as Brent can't help over-literally explaining his own and other people's jokes. The estate itself offers another consummately impersonal office building, the grey-blue grid of its exterior seeming more and more constrictive as we draw closer. All the while that doleful music continues; 'Handbags and Gladrags', like the visuals, establishes a melancholy mood then offers a hint of escape, clambering up the octaves with something like hope before tumbling all the way down just as the programme's title appears, plainly, over the final exterior shot.

But rather than the setting, it's *The Office*'s prizing of banality in behaviour that is most striking. Large parts of the show are characterised by people at their desks doing very little, the only soundtrack an ambient, soporific hum. (The DVD cannily uses this background murmur for its menu screens.) Merchant and Gervais went to considerable lengths to avoid anything that could be mistaken for excitement – as we have seen, general views offer not dynamic, informative compositions or characters

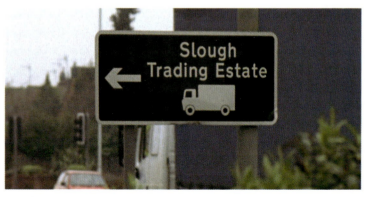

Uninviting, uninvolving, uninspiring: the credit sequence

engaged in purposeful activity but furniture or office equipment; a churning photocopier has a kind of metronomic rhythm, its constant activity always reproducing the same old thing, same old thing, same old thing, same old thing. When we do see people we often get the backs of their heads or otherwise Dawn dealing with a wrong number, Joan the cleaner emptying a bin, employees rubbing a bleary eye or yawning.

Wernham Hogg has the low-level mankiness of a real-life (rather than TV) office, shown through such details as Tim's sweaty pits as he shows off his dance moves or Brent's boss Jennifer's complaint about the smell in the lift. A character like Big Keith, so dry and deadpan as to suck life and air out of the room, epitomises this. This exchange with Tim about watching television, from I.v, is the nadir of office banter, inane commentary on inane activity, the tight framing making it all the more hellishly claustrophobic:

Keith: Just looking at a booklet at the moment?

Tim: Yeah.

Keith: What did you watch on telly last night?

59

Boring, isn't it? (I.v)

Tim: I didn't watch telly. I watched a video.

Keith: I watched that *Peak Practice*.

Tim: Yeah? I've never seen it.

Keith: Bloody repeat.

Tim: That's annoying, isn't it?

Keith: Not for me. I hadn't seen it.

[Pause]

Keith: Boring, isn't it? Just staying in and watching *Peak Practice* with your life.

Tim: Mmm. Yeah.

Keith: Not for me. I like it.

Tim [impatient]: Yeah, I just stayed in, had a big wank.

For Tim in particular, working life itself clearly feels like one long repeat.

Silence might seem a welcome alternative but this turns out to be even more excruciating, as when Tim and Lee stand together with nothing to say in I.i, or when a duff joke is greeted with indifference. The tendency of episodes to end on a downbeat note is perhaps the most extreme example of the programme's refusal to provide relief, to let us all laugh in an affirming, cathartic way. Initially this finds shape in the deflation of Brent's inane, insensitive pretensions: at the end of I.i, Dawn calls him a 'sad little man'; at the end of I.ii, having already dismissed him and his mates as 'seedy little men with seedy little jokes', Jennifer dismisses him as 'pathetic'; and in I.iii Brent and Finch's bitterness over their defeat in the company quiz prompts young temp Ricky to call them 'a couple of sad little men'. These notes of contempt, to which Brent has no response, have the effect of lending him a morsel of sympathy at the moment of his greatest crassness and fallibility, denying us the uncomplicated pleasure of pure ridicule. I.iii, I.iv and I.v conclude with dejection or embarrassment for Tim, the most sympathetic character. The first series itself ends with events that could be framed as a positive reinforcement of the previously threatened *status quo* – the Slough branch will stay afloat, Tim won't be leaving – but are instead presented in unremittingly downbeat fashion, leaving us downcast rather than uplifted. The second series offers little respite: II.i closes with Lee shoving Tim against the wall, II.ii leaves Dawn trapped with a self-pitying Brent blowing into a bottle; II.iii ends with Brent killing the mood at Trudy's birthday party with a grotesque sexual mime; and the series closes with the most depressing bathos of all as Brent's sacking is confirmed and Tim's second pass at Dawn ends in deflated humiliation.

Yet, despite the apparent insufferability of life at Wernham Hogg, it actually does matter to its employees, most of whom are caught in a double bind, disdaining the environment but with little alternative source of social nourishment. With the exception of the grim outing to Chaser's nightclub, the first series offers barely a glimpse outside the office building (the quiz night and end-of-year party are held in a downstairs function room), other than the mildly mocking aeroplane we see reflected in the window as Tim contemplates quitting in I.iv. The second series offers more exteriors (a fire drill, a lunchtime pub excursion, Brent's motivational speaking gig and Comic Relief photo call) but these too are work-related. As the first series ends, Tim and Gareth express real concern at the thought of losing their favourite colleagues, Dawn and Brent – and for us as viewers the emotional engagement also proves surprisingly substantial.

A crucial factor in this is the plausibility of the show's setting, the ease with which viewers used to the office environment could identify with Wernham Hogg compared to the more stylised workplaces more usually presented in TV sitcoms. However, the fostering of emotional engagement is achieved not merely through the show's naturalistic setting but, equally crucially, through its faux-documentary style. Although *The Office*'s creators were keen to avoid making the filming process the subject of humour in itself, the approach

nonetheless makes for a different viewing experience from the
conventional sitcom, with implications for both characters' behaviour
and viewer response.

The docusoap effect

Why the formal apparatus of docusoap should turn out to be so well-
suited to a sitcom is not perhaps immediately obvious: one, after all, is a
form of factual programming, ostensibly a subsection of the
observational documentary; the other a highly formalised comedy
format associated with a studio setting. In fact, over the past decade
both documentary and sitcom have been changing in ways that make it
harder to tell them apart, documentary seeking to ape the hermetic
milieu, simplistic characterisation and easily digestible plotting of
sitcom, sitcom trying to co-opt the seriality, associability and
'authenticity' of docusoap.

62   It's worth considering the ascent of the docusoap in some
detail. Researchers like Jon Dovey have suggested how the decline of
omniscient narration and institutional subjects – previously
cornerstones of TV observational documentary – has been matched by
the rise of more personalised content, either through the film-maker
undertaking an 'intrusion of individual identity'[10] into the programme
(the production procedures of Nick Broomfield, Michael Moore and
Louis Theroux, for instance, feature prominently as subjects of their
own films) or through concentration on individuals viewed without
reference to their broader social, political or economic context. In
identifying the docusoap as 'another new genre that foregrounds the
performance of individual identities',[11] Dovey points up its distinction
from earlier 'reality' shows such as COPS (1989–) in America or 999
Lifesavers (1994–) in the UK, whose 'authentic' aesthetic provided a fig-
leaf for the often exploitative selection of footage and stories that
tapped into contemporary fears over crime. Though less dramatic in
nature, the docusoap also thrived on the glamorisation of everyday

events, but by concentrating on individual participants, programme-makers were able to apply the same codes of 'authenticity' (natural lighting, hand-held camerawork sometimes 'surprised' by the action etc) to cheaper, easier subject matter that proved to have an equally substantial appeal.

Understood as a fly-on-the-wall observational documentary based around a specific location and tracing across a prolonged period the everyday experiences of a limited cast of 'ordinary' people, the docusoap format has plenty of precedents, most famously Paul Watson's series, *The Family* (BBC1, 1974, inspired by *An American Family*, PBS, 1972) and *Sylvania Waters* (BBC1, 1993), which focused on private families in Reading and Sydney respectively, introducing to documentary-making many of the pleasures of soap opera (the latter was widely described as the 'real-life *Neighbours*'). In the 1990s, however, the format came into its own. Molly Dineen's 1993 BBC2 series *The Ark*, about London Zoo, concentrated on the personal stories within an institutional setting (Dineen went on to make *In The Company of Men*, 1995, about the Welsh Guards, and highly personalised portrait films of Tony Blair and Geri Halliwell). Then in 1996, *The House*, about the renovation of the Royal Opera House, became an unexpected ratings success for BBC2 after viewers cottoned on to the corrosive office politics simmering within the venerable outfit. Similarly framed programmes about the church (*The Calling*, 1998) and the Ministry of Defence (*Defence of the Realm*, 1996) proved popular too and demonstrated a new tack in documentary-making. At a basic level, these were observational documentaries about great public institutions, and therefore continuous with the established traditions of British TV documentary-making. What was new was their emphasis on individuality; rather than proposing an argument about the function or role of such institutions in national life, they foregrounded the words and behaviour of strong characters who were entertaining in their own right. Like the emergency service-based reality shows before them, they were less concerned with 'the outer world' than with 'inner stories' – individualised tales of the effects of injury or

crime, the trials of a day at work. It was a shift from argument engaging
the brain to entertainment engaging the emotions; as John Corner puts
it, 'the viewing invitation slides from the dynamics of understanding to
the . . . transaction of vicarious witness and empathy'.[12] Audience
conceptions of factual viewing underwent a concomitant shift: Brian
Winston suggested that docusoap's appeal relied on 'its inversion of
public expectations of the documentary . . . The associative nexus of the
word "documentary" itself, "worthy", "dull", "intelligent" and
"serious" programming, was blown away by the docusoaps' fixation
on the trivial, the everyday and the ordinary.'[13] Rather than giving us
an argument about the way we live today or even an ever-changing
roster of everyday heroes to appreciate, as their emergency services-
based predecessors did, these programmes offered regular characters
audiences could associate with, or feel affectionately superior to:
hopeless trainee drivers, unapologetic traffic wardens. Banality became
the new escapism.

Docusoap offered the added bonus of characters being able to
express their fears and aspirations directly to the camera, either *in situ*
or in the form of 'talking heads'. This new directness of approach
indicated the major formal shift of docusoap compared to conventional
observation documentary: the wholesale embrace of the camera. In
many respects this was a welcome development, rejecting the implicit
view of the shooting process as a dirty little secret, an unfortunate
practical necessity rather than the fundamental motor of the situation.
If the Broomfield-Moore-Theroux approach acknowledged the camera
as a tool of power, shifting the balance of control away from their
politician-businessman-celebrity subjects and towards the film-maker,
docusoap aimed for a cosier approach, presenting the camera as a friend
to whom subjects could open up in confidence – as Keith Beattie notes,
it 'lends the format to varieties of conversation and confession'.[14] *The
Cruise*'s (1998) Jane MacDonald, for instance, was often seen chatting
to director Chris Terrill in the confessional mode otherwise associated
with video diaries or talk shows, or as if to a girlfriend ('What do you
think, Chris?' she once asked while shopping for pants). This new

64

approach inevitably ran the risk of encouraging exhibitionism. 'The presence of the camera,' Dovey notes, 'elicits mediated versions of self. More than ever the docusoap illustrates the principle that any documentary is primarily a record of the relationship between the film-makers and the subjects.'[15] At worst, it provided an excuse for wannabes to revel in the gaze of the lens, a dynamic that found its logical extension in the institutionalised exhibitionism of the *Big Brother*-style reality show. But at its most affecting, this new openness offered an unmediated rapport between subject and audience that made emotional association central to factual programming as never before: it was now possible to empathise, not just sympathise.

The inherent appeal of real life could now be structured according to conventional modes of narrative entertainment, selecting participants for their screen appeal, as if casting for a soap or drama, and situations for their predictable longevity and potential for low-level conflict and minor incident. Indeed, many docusoaps were promoted more like fiction than fact, with the stress on character and plot: *The Cruise*, for instance, boasted glamorous opening credits ('Starring . . .') and story-so-far synopses, and was scheduled to alternate with *EastEnders* (1985–); the widespread use of chummy voice-over and incidental music further sweetened the actuality pill. Most important was the shoe-horning of supposedly unmediated reality into narrative shapes to which audiences were accustomed, maximising through selective editing and excitable narration the potential suspense or entertainment value of any given situation. MTV's *The Real World* (1992) was a precursor of both docusoap and *Big Brother*-style reality programming, with a dozen young subjects extensively filmed in their shared house and daily lives. Producer Mary-Ellis Bunim told *Time* magazine that each episode used three writers to whittle the hours of footage down to a conventional narrative structure – 'we storyboard each scene, just like a prime-time series'.[16] Where *The Real World* placed a premium on emotional drama, however, British docusoaps' stress on humorous banter and good-natured, long-suffering professionalism was more in tune with light entertainment.

If, then, docusoap is seen as reliant on humour, emotional engagement and simplistic narrative – usually involving a temporary challenge to the *status quo* – its distance from sitcom begins to look rather small. Indeed, the overlap has been used as a stick with which to beat both forms. The producer of another, fancier kind of new observational documentary, Channel 4's *Smart Hearts*, could complain that by the time that show went out in August 2000 'a decade of "factual entertainment" had created a culture of viewers and critics who had grown used to a cast of happy losers prepared to let their lives descend into sitcom farce'.[17] Dovey notes that in docusoap 'the characters do not change or develop: they are "cast" for a particular set of two-dimensional qualities which they continue to act out over and over (like characters in a bad sitcom).'[18] He also observes that 'a number of successful docusoaps occupied territory that had previously been the setting for successful sitcoms: *Hotel* was a kind of documentary equivalent of *Fawlty Towers*, *Pleasure Beach* is not so far away from the holiday camp sitcom *Hi-De-Hi*, and *The Cruise* carried strong echoes of the US series from the late 1970s *The Love Boat*.'[19] Paul Watson, maker of *The Family* and *Sylvania Waters*, concurred: 'They are comedy, made so often because our comedy has gone off the boil.'[20] Bernard Clark also suggests 'it was the collapse of traditional entertainment, especially situation comedy on BBC1, which led to the explosion of docusoaps'.[21]

Mainstream British situation comedy was indeed in parlous shape at the time. Sitcom was, however, thriving in the US; correspondingly, docusoap never achieved the same order of success there and its eventual development cleaved even more closely to the sitcom model than its British counterpart; it was there that the membrane between the genres was most porous, largely by gearing series around 'real' people who were already famous as performers. The best known, MTV's *The Osbournes*, was explicitly presented in sitcom style, with credits featuring a perky theme tune and caricatured versions of the family harking back to 50s' sitcoms based around fictionalised variants of star personae, such as *Make Room for Daddy* and *I Love*

Lucy (1955).[22] Shows like *The Simple Life* (2002–) and *Newlyweds: Nick and Jessica* (2003–) continue this approach.

The Office's wholesale adoption of the docusoap format, then, represents not genre pastiche but the reclamation for situation comedy of formal tropes developed by factual programme-makers in the (successful) hope of emulating sitcom's appeal. If *The Office*'s premium on naturalism made it harder to get laughs from 'big' farcical set-ups, overtly wacky characterisations or conspicuously sharp-witted dialogue, the co-option of docusoap's formal trappings on their own terms brought tools of emotional engagement not available to the conventional sitcom writer. *The Office* was able to bring the more direct empathetic appeals of the factual format to bear on its fictional characters, resulting in an intimacy and strength of association of unusual potency in a sitcom. The plausibility of Wernham Hogg as a workplace – both in terms of its physical environment and the relative lack of exaggeration in the depiction of characters and events based there – resonated sympathetically with viewers used to comparable situations in their lives but not on their screens, and created a predisposition to view the action as more 'real'. (Indeed, some viewers apparently took it for the real thing: 'I sat through most of the first series and thought it was a real docusoap', one viewer posted on a TV discussion website.)[23] Correspondingly, audiences were more alert than usual to the emotional consequences of behaviour, from the minor irritations of a fussy deskmate to the threat of job losses. Most affecting in this vein are scenes where characters verge on tears: Dawn at the end of the first episode, Gareth at the end of the first series, Brent at the end of the second series. What would appear jarring in a conventional sitcom achieves significant impact both through the plausibility of the context and because factual entertainment has trained us to appreciate tears as the ultimate index of the authentic, supposed proof of the subject's unguarded relationship with the camera and audience – the reality TV money shot. *Nurses*, *Lakesiders* and *Airport*, for instance, all had principals breaking down[24] while the success of the first series of *Big*

67

Brother was cemented by the sight of 'Nasty' Nick Bateman blubbing when his machinations were revealed.

The use of the camera

Perhaps the most potent mode by which the docusoap – and *The Office* – engenders audience empathy is the direct address to the camera and, by extension, the audience. Without the comforting distance provided by the 'fourth wall', our implication in a given situation is of a much higher order – when a character talks to or even glances at the camera we become part of that exchange. If it's an embarrassing conversation we share in the mortification; if it's an emotional crisis we feel invested in its outcome. Elsewhere, 'talking head' interviews allow characters to express inner feelings about their personal and professional lives more directly than would be plausibly possible in the context of everyday working life, providing a window onto their hopes, concerns and frustrations and thus increasing our investment in their circumstances. It is in the explicit use of the camera that *The Office*'s marriage of factual aesthetics with fictional content yields its most potent results.

This isn't to suggest that *The Office*'s characters are aware of the presence of the camera in every shot; there are moments where Merchant and Gervais short-cut this dynamic by using 'spycam' footage, supposedly clandestine observations signified by subtle codes hinting at 'undercover' shooting, usually involving a visual barrier between the camera and the subject – potentially something as simple as out-of-focus desktop equipment in the foreground – to give the impression that the subjects are further away than usual. Perhaps the most frequently used such symbol are the Venetian blinds hanging in the windows separating Brent's office or the meeting room from the main office space; it's through these that we witness the grotesque sight of Brent applying a magazine sample of aftershave and trying out supposedly coquettish poses before interviewing Karen in I.v, or his humiliating dressings-down by Neil, or Tim's declaration of his feelings for Dawn in II.vi; similarly, our views of Dawn and Lee arguing in I.iv are through the wire-mesh grid inside panes of fortified glass in the doors leading to the stairwell. As well as setting up a visual impediment, these lines contribute to the feeling of constriction and entrapment in the office, as if the characters are caged for our entertainment.

In general, however, the camera is evidently part of the dynamic it records. Sometimes this has almost physical expression, when the camera echoes or reinforces our discomfort through the simple tack of zooming slightly out, as if backing away from moments of supreme embarrassment: Brent and Gareth leaving Brenda in her wheelchair halfway down a stairwell during the fire drill in II.ii; Brent stunned at his own tactlessness after telling a large woman at the Christmas party how relieved he is that she isn't his blind date. Yet

69

The cage effect (I.iv)

even as the camera recoils, Brenda's and Brent's eyes respectively stay fixed on it, daring us to look away, as if from a beggar on the street. There are distancing long shots too, when the camera appears to have already retreated as far as possible into the furthest available corner, as if to keep the situation at arm's length. This is most often used to sharpen the discomfort as an episode concludes: Brent, Dawn and Ricky are left marooned in the middle of the meeting room after the fake sacking in I.i; Brent, Jennifer and Neil sit similarly stranded after the real sacking at the end of II.vi; Brent stands alone backstage at the end of the first part of the Christmas Specials. Sometimes the camera's presence is made almost obscenely obvious, as on the repeated occasions when Gordon, the maintenance man (played by Merchant's father Ron), gazes straight at the lens. Transfixed as if by a predator or stage fright, his profoundly disruptive presence reminds us that all the characters are at least aware of and probably performing for the lens – an inference made explicit in the Christmas Special, with the characters discussing how they came across in the broadcast of the original series.

There are varying responses to the fact of being filmed. Finchy, Glynn and IT engineer Simon, for instance, look confidently to the camera after telling jokes, while (to Brent's particular embarrassment) Donna makes a point of including the camera in her broadcast of the fact that she slept with someone from the office in I.v. She also appeals to it in her compulsory health-and-safety training session with Gareth in the same episode, at first rolling her eyes at it, then mortified that it should catch her in such demeaning positions, being instructed on how to lift a little box. Afterwards, to cover his own embarrassment, Gareth shows the camera his clipboard (he gave her an 'A'). Elsewhere, the camera is seen as the site of dispute for characters who compete for its approval or sympathy – in I.vi, Brent winks at it after revealing how he 'cheated medical science', then Malcolm fixes it with a sceptical pout; when Neil is introduced in II.i, he and Brent have a minor verbal scuffle for control of the camera.

Across the series, it is obvious that the character who takes his

Gordon transfixed (II.vi)

relationship with the camera most seriously is David Brent: if he isn't 71
actually playing up to it, he's keeping a beady eye out, never letting a
human interaction take precedence over his relationship with the lens.
At moments of personal pleasure or triumph – hiring Karen as his
secretary in I.v, being offered promotion in I.vi – Brent turns to the
camera to share his unvarnished delight. When his inhibitions are at
their lowest – when he's drunk at Chasers nightclub – he simply,
honestly mugs, demanding its attention like a kid showing off. Over the
course of the second series, Gervais and Merchant provide more and
more opportunities for Brent to perform set-pieces that fall
embarrassingly flat, and it's usually to the camera that he appeals for
support (the desperate rictus that concludes his disastrous welcoming
speech in II.i, the triumphalist finger he jabs at the lens at the end of his
infamous dance routine in II.v). When inescapably caught out, as during
that very first phone conversation in front of Alex, he squirms on the
pin, fixing the lens with that look of panicked, hopeless defiance, lips
drawn back and teeth bared in a mirthless, defensive mask.

Constantly, acutely preoccupied with how he comes across, Brent is also disastrously ill equipped to assess and modify his behaviour – a tension summed up in his repeated attempts to pay lip service to political correctness without changing his conduct accordingly. Brent's confused attempts to impress several different groups at one time – to fulfil contradictory expectations within the same exchange – are compounded by the presence of the camera, representing another audience he is constantly trying to please. We have already seen how that very first scene with Alex the prospective forklift truck driver (a scene with which the taster tape and pilot also opened), offers Brent the chance to embarrass himself; comparably, the painful trip to the warehouse with Jennifer in I.ii sees him trying to be both professional manager and one of the lads, and be seen to be both by the camera, ultimately failing to impress on any of these levels. Elsewhere, consciously under observation by the camera, he visibly struggles with the temptation to look at Jennifer's legs, or internet pornography. II.iv

Doesn't that feel nice? (II.iv)

provides another instance of Brent's anxiety that the camera is recording an activity he feels faintly ashamed of. Following Brent's confrontation with Neil, Gareth starts massaging his shoulders, which he enjoys for a few moments before registering the homoerotic undertones the camera is dispassionately recording.

> **Brent:** What you doing?
>
> **Gareth:** You looked a bit tense.
>
> **Brent:** I am, with him.
>
> **Gareth:** Doesn't that feel nice?
>
> **Brent:** Yeah, but– [points at camera as if to say, 'what about them?']
>
> **Gareth:** Shall we do some more work on your abs?
>
> **Brent:** Not now.
>
> [Gareth starts doing a light chopping action on Brent's shoulders. Brent stares blankly into the camera.]

73

He also finds himself constantly trying to explain, mitigate or justify to the camera his mate Chris Finch's crude, non-PC humour, while being careful not to let Finch think he has anything less than respect and admiration for his talent. We only need to hear one side of this telephone conversation from I.iii:

> Finchy! Brent. All right? Don't forget tonight. Oh, here goes, straight away. Go on, go on. 'What's black and slides down Nelson's Column?' Don't know. 'Winnie Mandela'? I don't – Oh! Oh, yeah, that's good. No, it's not – No, it's not racist. No. Yeah, I thought – The column, 'cause he – And she is black. And she probably actually is married so it's not even libel. Yeah, seven. See you. Bye!

Gervais' performance at such moments is an impressively nuanced balancing act; we must register both Brent's awareness of his miscalculations and his attempts to conceal that awareness. The pleasures of his acting are congruent with our attitude towards the subjects of docusoaps or reality shows – we demand them to be 'genuine', 'real', 'not performing', yet relish moments in which they are 'revealed' to be performing for the camera.

Brent's use of the camera is symptomatic of his sustained attempts to promote his inflated view of himself, elsewhere expressed through a willingness to cut short, rewrite, ignore or imagine events. Like docusoap itself, he is determined to impose a shape that suits his purposes. One of the ways in which the factual format seeks to spin the dross of the daily grind into narrative gold is the use of a structuring voice-over which, although chummier than the 'voice of God' of old-school documentary, can in fact be more controlling, massaging potentially disruptive events to fit its narrative schema. Brent's constant running commentary on jokes and events is his basic means of exerting control, explaining gags and making sure the camera knows which things he disapproves of, cackling or tutting at it in an attempt to enlist its and our allegiance. He will try to steer a situation to fit his preconceptions and, if he fails, petulantly abort the exchange: on the training day in I.iv, when Rowan asks Keith his feelings about his job, Brent tries to answer for him; when the truth comes out ('this job's just a stop-gap, really, it's pretty brainless') Brent challenges and steamrollers Keith then changes the subject. Elsewhere he's caught out trying to present a false picture, as with his fake firings of Chris Finch and phantom employee 'Julie Anderton', or his climactic claim to have faked high blood pressure. Sometimes things turn out, in Brentworld, not really to have happened; having lost a quiz to Tim and Ricky in I.iii, Finch's lobbing Tim's shoes over the roof becomes, in Brent's eyes, 'the real quiz'.

If ever a record is being kept – other, that is, than the filming itself – he's careful to leave the right impression, as in I.vi, when he invites Tim to discuss his dissatisfaction with his job and asks Karen, his new PA, to take notes.

> **Brent:** I don't want to put words in your mouth, but what sort of boss would you say I am? 'I'm a –'?
>
> **Tim:** Good boss?
>
> **Brent:** Yep. [To Karen] Put down 'good', he said 'good'.
>
> **Tim:** No, mate, you're a great boss, but –
>
> **Brent [interrupts]:** 'Great.'

When the chat ends without Brent alleviating Tim's disillusionment, Brent sends him packing with instructions to keep the narrative to his liking: 'Don't say out there what you've said in here – apart from the thing about "good boss".' His interview with a trade journalist in II.vi follows a more extreme pattern of attempted shaping.

> **Helena:** Right, so would you like to tell me about your individual outlook on management?
>
> **Brent:** Sure. Put: 'David Brent is refreshingly laid-back for a man with such responsibility –'
>
> **Helena:** Yeah, can you just answer in your own words and I'll work it up later?
>
> **Brent:** Yeah. [Pause.] 'Brent mused and then replied –'
>
> **Helena:** Sorry, no. David, could you just say what's on your mind? I'm getting it down, so –
>
> **Brent:** Well, are you getting it down? Because you're not doing shorthand and I'm going to be pretty – [Snaps his fingers.]
>
> **Helena:** Just –
>
> **Brent:** Well, okay. Your question, I suppose, was: 'Is it difficult to remain authoritative and yet so popular?'
>
> **Helena:** Well, no, that wasn't my question.
>
> **Brent:** Well, shall I answer that one first?[25]

75

Brent's concern for control of his self-image is also evident in his use of stills cameras, an approach developed over the second series. (In the first, his Polaroid portraiture of secretarial candidates Karen and Stuart hints at his attitude: the blonde is treated to a carefully set-up shot, the bloke an off-hand, ill-timed snap.) When Neil arrives at Slough, Brent is careful to leave lying around an old copy of *Inside Paper* magazine bearing his image, while his foray into motivational speaking is seen as another opportunity to strike a pose: when Ray takes a snap for the agency website Brent adopts a series of starlet-style postures ludicrously at odds with his actual appearance. Appearance in front of a second lens is used to compound Brent's worst moments of humiliation: immediately after being given his marching orders in II.v he trudges downstairs in ostrich costume to face the local paper's snapper; and when, in II.vi, even his hopes of a career in motivational speaking are dashed and he petulantly orders Ray, Jude and reporter Helena out of his office, Helena prolongs the agony by asking to take a couple of shots – for which Brent, ever the professional, adopts an off-the-peg pensive, thumb-on-chin look. He even sends optimistically produced fan glossies to the dating agency he joins in the Christmas Special.

The talking head provides a further tool for shaping meaning through explicit use of the camera. For Brent it's the major opportunity to construct his persona, expound his philosophy and also demonstrate his self-ignorance: his pompous inanities are delivered with a smug heavy-lidded blink and self-satisfied smirk, holding the camera's gaze all the while. His talk is punctuated with imaginary reports of praise: 'People say I'm the best boss'; 'I get all this: "Ooh, David, you're a brilliant singer–songwriter" '; 'People watching [me and Finchy] will go: "Why is that funny?" and we'll tell them why and they'll go: "Oh, yeah, yeah, yeah. You are the best." It's their opinion.' In II.iii he tells an employee 'Most people think I look about thirty.' 'Definitely not,' the employee says. 'Oh,' Brent snaps, 'are you calling them liars?' Having narrowly avoided lynching at the end of the first series he offers his crowning self-delusion, resplendent in his self-coddling hypocrisy:

Brent says 'cheese' (II.iv, II.v)

You've seen how I react to people. I make them feel good, make them think that anything's possible. If I make them laugh along the way, sue me. And I don't do it so they'll turn around and go: 'Ooh, thank you, David, for the opportunity, thank you for the wisdom, thank you for the laughs.' I do it so one day someone'll go: 'There goes David Brent. I must remember to thank him.'

Equally indicative is the talking head from II.v in which Brent hints at his aspirations towards a showbiz career.

You've seen me entertain and raise money but maybe I'd like to do that in the future for a living – you know, use my humour and my profile to both help and amuse people. And if it's ideas for TV shows, game shows or whatever you want, I'm your man. I'm already exploring the entertainment avenue with my management training, but I'd like to do that on a global scale, really.

This comes as no surprise. For Brent, everything is an opportunity to explore the 'entertainment avenue', from tours of the office with fresh meat unused to his comedic assaults to employee pep talks that develop into unwished-for serenades, not to mention the infamous dance routine in II.v. The transformation of a teamwork seminar into an impromptu *Unplugged* session in I.iv is a case study in his attempted dual performance of the roles of good boss and chilled-out entertainer – the former none too subtly undercut from the start as we see him discussing his care for his employees' welfare ('If they've got a problem, I've got a problem') while Dawn sobs unheeded in the background. The second series offers several opportunities for Brent to frame business exercises as showbiz escapades, much as Gervais' character Clive did in 'Golden Years': 'Enjoy the show,' he tells Neil before a group meeting in II.ii; 'I love being backstage,' he giggles before the motivational talk in II.iv. He even imagines himself to be part of the production process rather than its subject: 'I think you're mad to let me and Finchy on the bleeding telly,' he says in I.iii, 'you'll only be able to use about twenty per cent of it when you get me and him together'; after spouting some meretricious self-promotion about his charity work in the Comic Relief episode, II.v, he runs his hand across the bottom of the shot suggesting 'Put a number up there, shall we, if people wanna make donations?' The emails included in the script book demonstrate Brent's eagerness to sit in on the editing process and, just before losing his job in II.vi, he is working on a game show proposal.

Brent's unabashed view of his participation in the docusoap as a springboard to a career in light entertainment reflects a kind of death of deference in the observational documentary – the new credo is ask not what you can do for the camera, ask what the camera can do for you. John Corner notes

> the degree of self-consciousness now often displayed by the participants in observational sequences. This self-display is no longer viewable as an attempt to feign natural behaviour but is taken as a performative opportunity in its own right. As such it constitutes a staple element of docusoap in contrast with the self-restrained naturalism of demeanour, speech, and behaviour in classic observationalism.[26]

Brent is misguided about his personal talent rather than the potential of his situation, as the post-docusoap entertainment careers of the likes of Jeremy Spake (*Airport*) and Jane MacDonald (*The Cruise*) show. 'Love Lottery', the *Blind Date*-style nightclub show in the first Christmas Special, allies Brent – now established within the series as a love-to-hate-him docusoap character – with two real-life micro-celebrities, 'Bubble' from that year's *Big Brother* and Howard Brown, the Halifax employee featured in the building society's advertising. None, it's probably fair to say, would have been able to exercise a claim to professional celebrity a generation ago. To be filmed becomes validation in itself, Brent's last, best defence against abuse: when taunted in the street, 'I go: "Yeah? What have you ever done on telly?

Nothing. So don't –" '; and when 'Love Lottery' contestant Kim asks 'Who the fuck's that?' he snaps back: 'Who are *you*? What have you been on before? Nothing. So don't –'

It's only in the Christmas Specials that Brent himself has to acknowledge the gulf between his self-conception and his appearance to others that has been obvious to the other characters, and the basis of the humour to the audience, throughout the previous two series. We learn how devastated he has been by their broadcast, labelling it 'a stitch-up' and for a while persisting in the promotion of his pretentious cod-glamorous self-image through a self-funded pop single – a cover version of 'If You Don't Know Me By Now' – whose consummately clichéd video demonstrates his continued lack of self-knowledge. 'You didn't see me in there with her,' Brent assured employees of his initial meeting with Jennifer about the redundancies back at in I.i, but of course by now everyone – including Brent himself – has had the opportunity to see that very unimpressive exchange, merely one of the myriad hypocrisies laid bare by the lens. Yet despite his evident sense of betrayal, Brent is unable to shake his desire to impress the camera. Its following him even after his departure from Wernham Hogg seems to confirm his celebrity status and, more pitifully, to represent his only persistent social bond. When Brent is at his most disillusioned, drunk in a motel room, it's to the camera he turns to air his grievances, in an uncomfortably intimate sequence (reminiscent of a section from Louis Theroux's profile of Jimmy Savile, where the subject let his guard down and revealed rather too much).

It's only after meeting and being reassured by his blind date, Carol – who, crucially, has never seen Brent on TV – that we sense a change in Brent's outlook. After he sees Carol to her cab, his glances back seem geared around her more than the camera, to which he throws a newly open, uningratiating look. For the first time he isn't cravenly dependent on the approval of others, dismissing Finch and Neil and larking about in front of the camera in an unprecedentedly unself-conscious (if no less attention-seeking) way; as the party draws to a close he tries once again to marshall a stills camera, but this time

Lover and confidant: Brent's faith in the camera holds firm (Christmas Special, Part One, Part Two)

it's for sentimental rather than self-promoting reasons, asking for a group shot of 'the old gang'. Our very last glimpse of Wernham Hogg sees Brent, in talking head, asking the crew 'Have you got everything you need? Cheers.' He gets up and leaves an empty seat, the rustling noise of his mic drawing attention to the recording media he is finally choosing to ignore. At last it's possible to imagine him being indifferent to his image, recognising that – as Tim says shortly before – 'If you turn the camera off ... I'm still here, my life's not over.'

Although Brent takes his relationship with the camera more seriously than the other leads, their interactions with it are also illustrative of their characters. Their talking heads, for instance, reveal facets that can only be hinted at or observed in passing in the context of the action proper. Gareth's confirm how few mental steps away from sheer militaristic lunacy he is at any one time, leaping from email porn investigation to poisonous frogs (with the conclusion that 'I could catch a monkey'), from a Slough nightclub to untreated gangrene, from hypothetical office romance to the threat of gays in the trenches. Tim and Dawn, meanwhile, use it in the same wittily self-deprecating way, sarcastically bemoaning the state of their professional or personal lives; their confessions of frustration provide relief, not just to them but to us as viewers, confirming our perceptions of the awfulness of the situation. If watching the talking heads is comparable to engaging the characters in conversation, Brent and Gareth have you searching for an excuse to leave; with Tim and Dawn you can share the pain.

Whereas Brent sees the camera as something to show off to, for Gareth it is more of a potential accuser: he eyes it suspiciously when coming into the office in I.iii and guiltily gets back to work when it catches him stretching chewing gum out of his mouth. He very rarely engages with it directly, perhaps stealing a shy glance or two when showing off about a big night out or his Territorial Army escapades. The camera's presence illuminates a larger part of Gareth's character: his vulnerability, the anxiety and insecurity that conceivably lie at the

Stop making sense

root of his military obsession. Preoccupied with surveillance as he is, being observed himself makes him uneasy: he is at his happiest when he can turn the meeting room into a foxhole in his temporary roles as porn investigator or quiz deviser; when it comes to sex we learn that in his ultimate fantasy 'I'm just watching' (I.iv). In II.ii he reassures Lee that any fears over Tim and Dawn's relationship are unfounded: 'I've been watching him like a hawk.' Most of his (non-sexual) fantasies revolve around defence from outlandish attack – he can easily imagine Japanese sniper fire as a clear and present danger. If the camera represents a potential threat, however, it can also denote an objective observer to whom Gareth can appeal: after he fails to notice Tim disappearing from behind the stack of files he erects between their desks in I.i, Gareth can maintain 'I'm not talking to myself because they're filming.'

Merchant and Gervais suggest that the fundamentally unsympathetic characterisation of Dawn's fiancé, Lee, is also a function of camera presence. Lee is a bit of a problem; he and Dawn have an established rather than a passionate relationship, one which (the writers confirm) dates back to adolescence; we must presume that they share at least some opinions and happy memories. It seems a shame, though, that we never see him being nice to her. Merchant says that with the love triangle they were aiming for a dynamic closer to *Casablanca* than *Titanic* – 'a decision between two good men . . . a real dramatic dilemma' rather than the rivalry of a hero and 'a twirly moustached maniac' – but it's hard to muster any sympathy for Lee; there are so many well-observed moments of boorish insensitivity and nothing to counterbalance it. Merchant concedes that 'we don't give him enough screen time to mount his case because we want people to side with Tim' but also recalls

84

wanting to suggest that [Lee is] a little bit uncomfortable with the camera being around. He's got one eye on how his mates are going to watch this, and he's not going to be touchy-feely and sensitive on camera, he's going to do that in the privacy of his own living room. That's not for his mates to see, that's not for anyone else to see. As far as anyone else is concerned he's a bloke and you don't piss around.

Tim, meanwhile, treats the camera neither as an audience to play to nor a challenge to be warily guarded against, but as a welcome witness, even a friend. His mode is conversational rather than competitive and it's this that really socialises us into the situation and confirms him as our proxy – we share his amusement when he shows us the signs Gareth makes for his temporary office door, his embarrassment when he turns to us in the silence after one of Brent's gags falls flat. Like Brent, he regularly fixes the camera with a look that says 'Are you getting this?' but where Brent's hungry eyes ask 'Isn't this great?' Tim's deadpan mask pleads 'Isn't this awful? Pity me. Help me.' There's a moment, after Brent has berated Gareth for 'stealing' his jokes in I.iii, when the camera pans to Tim and, briefly, he pulls a face right at it – a mask of almost hysterical frustration that no other character sees – and in that moment uses his relationship with the camera to establish a bond that implicitly unites character and audience in opposition to the situation in which Tim is stranded. The bond is reinforced in I.iv: when we first see Brent playing his guitar, Tim comes over to address the camera, telling us 'he went home to get it'. This is not to suggest that Tim is indifferent to how he comes across (when Dawn turns him down at the end of the training day episode, his first embarrassed look is to the camera; he turns to it self-consciously again after Lee has shoved him away from Dawn in II.i) but it doesn't dictate or forestall his actions in the way it might Brent's or Gareth's.

Except, that is, in one fundamental area: his relationship with Dawn. An office flirtation requires discretion and tact at the best of times, but when the workplace is being filmed to boot, such necessity is magnified by several orders. The developing romance between Tim and Dawn emerges over the course of the series from an incidental detail to the focus of the whole narrative: the considerable audience anticipation preceding the Christmas Specials was based at least as much – if not more – on whether the pair would finally get together as it was on discovering Brent's post-Wernham Hogg fortunes. The emotional weight this relationship achieved is, along with the credible moments of tearful breakdown, *The Office*'s most impressive achievement in terms of characterisation, and stems from the two sides of the docusoap dynamic: on the one hand, the format's direct emotional appeal offers a more powerful plausibility than a conventional sitcom could; on the other, the presence of the camera within the situation enforces an understated subtlety in the development of the romance. To an unusual degree, Tim and Dawn's varying feelings for one another – which cannot be expressed explicitly – are intimated through looks and gazes,

Tim turns to the camera as Brent berates Gareth (I.iii), when Brent gets his guitar (I.iv) and after being shoved by Lee (II.i)

a hesitant courtship played out under the camera's eye rather than through dialogue. As Merchant says,

> because the camera's filming them they can't show their emotions, they can't show their true feelings. So it's almost like some kind of Victorian seething melodrama where just his touching her or her touching him, that becomes as much as a kiss, it means that much.

Gervais paraphrases: 'A look became a touch, a touch became a kiss, a kiss became a shag.'

To begin with, Tim and Dawn's is an amicable, light-hearted flirtation grounded in workplace banter and shared despair at Brent's and Gareth's shortcomings – little things, but regular and consistent enough to establish theirs as the programme's only bond based on affection, support and a shared outlook. It's his successful comforting of her after her fight with Lee – offset by her announcement that she's thinking of leaving – that encourages Tim to make his move in I.iv, inviting her out for a drink but being humiliatingly told that 'I haven't split up with him'. Despite the knockback we can see how unsettled Dawn is by the possibility and how awkward both feel in each other's company afterwards – especially given the public nature of Tim's overture and the fact that the episode becomes common knowledge around the office in no time. Their awkwardness is illustrated by stilted conversations of no more or less banality than usual, but played in a stiffly self-conscious rather than casually flirtatious key. The subtlety of Martin Freeman and Lucy Davis's performances make plain both characters' regret at the situation; obliged to be in one another's company, they are denied any way of communicating meaningfully without either being under scrutiny from colleagues and the camera or arousing suspicion. Yet there is plainly no hostility on either side; their persistent affection is expressed through shots of each gazing in turn at the other as they go about their business, unnoticed by the object of the look or anyone else but the camera. Eventually, after another stilted exchange, Dawn makes the small, big gesture of brushing her hand against Tim's shoulder – an unexpectedly touching and powerful movement that underlines the intensity of the camera's oppression.[27]

The look remains an important mode of communication in the second series. Dawn is plainly mortified when Rachel asks Tim out in front of her in II.ii but Tim noticeably, tacitly appeals to Dawn for her approval or opinion, glancing across at her before accepting the invitation; she is unresponsive. Rather than looks, Tim and Rachel's relationship is established through equally subtle but telling physical contact – the occasional chuck under the chin or, most notably, the moment during Trudy's birthday celebrations in II.iii when the camera notices Tim's hand lighting on her waist and her hand meeting his, unobserved by the colleagues with whom they are chatting. This remains a facet of Tim and Dawn's relationship: in II.iv, as she prepares to accompany Brent on his public-speaking gig, they have a slightly forced chat that ends with another brushed hand, this time ending in a brief handclasp, the potentially disruptive effects of which are forestalled by Brent's appearance in preposterous 'yoof' garb. The Comic Relief

88

The missed gaze (I.v)

The handclasp (II.iv)

episode, II.v, contains an unexpectedly powerful kiss between the two, purportedly for the purposes of Dawn's sponsored activity. Though far briefer and more chaste than the kiss Tim and Rachel share the previous episode, the subtly established low register of Tim and Dawn's interaction built up over ten episodes loads this with an emotional impact of a far higher order that leaves both characters shaken and pensive well into the next episode, whose smoking-room group discussion on romance sees Dawn very conspicuously avoiding looking at Tim.

Another tiny gesture – Dawn's flicking the back of Tim's neck – prompts him to describe in a talking head his feelings for her: 'under different circumstances then sure, something may have happened, but she's going away now, you can't act – You can't change circumstances, you know.' He rethinks this, and sets in motion one of *The Office*'s most radical formal episodes: for the first time a talking head is disrupted, its subject revealed not to be a disengaged superego commenting from afar but a person sat in another room in the same environment. As the camera shakily follows, Tim strides down a corridor towards Dawn's desk and asks to talk to her in the meeting room. This done, he removes his microphone and their conversation proceeds in silence. Not just a tactic for building suspense – which it achieves with terrific success – this also underlines the fundamental differences between Brent's approach to being filmed and Tim's; the latter is able to prioritise other concerns, and also perhaps has the self-awareness to have learned from the embarrassment of asking Dawn out on camera previously, in I.iv. Viewing the conversation through Venetian blinds, with nothing on the soundtrack but the ambient rustling of the mic against Tim's pocket lining, we are made to feel for the first time like *bona fide* voyeurs; Tim's previous behaviour has succeeded in establishing a link between him and us against Brent and Gareth, but now he severs this, privileging his and Dawn's privacy in a manner antithetical to the entire docusoap project. It's an audacious move that makes gripping viewing out of a half-seen, unheard exchange that ends in an ambiguous hug. Again making explicit the operation of technology in the situation, Tim returns to his desk and holds the mic to his mouth, restoring the link. 'She said no, by the way.' His voice is too loud, like someone talking in your ear; too painful, like something casually swatted to death.

We have seen how Gervais and Merchant worried that in sending Dawn to Florida they had short-circuited their own narrative before realising that as 'documentary teams interfere' they could simply have the crew within the programme offer to fly Dawn and Lee home. Aside from its convenience, the tactic further underlines the presence of the camera within Dawn and Tim's relationship; but where previously its demands had resulted in unwanted stress, here it alters the dynamic in a beneficial way. Had the characters not appeared in a documentary, they would never have ended up together. It's only in the second part of the Christmas Specials that Dawn returns to Wernham Hogg, in a sequence whose form expressively reflects the characters' feelings. In accordance with their stringent pursuit of plausibility, Gervais and Merchant have one camera crew following Dawn, another already *in situ* in the office. We intercut between Dawn's progress through the building and Tim going about his work, an unusual tactic in the

Tim asks Dawn, again (II.vi). 'She said no, by the way'

Dawn's visit to Wernham Hogg (Christmas Special, Part Two)

programme; gradually the cameras' ranges intersect, Tim's ears pricking up when a colleague is heard to say 'Oh, my God!' The office camera pans round and, like Tim, we can't quite get a clear view of Dawn, our anticipation whetted by her emerging from behind a pillar into a field of employees who crowd to greet her. Dawn's camera shows that her view of Tim is similarly obscured, a literal, physical illustration of the work context that has always formed a barrier between them. Like her attention, her camera zeroes in on Tim even as she banters away politely to the others; he gets up, a smile on his face, and wanders to the group's periphery; they don't exchange a word, but their looks move from

recognition to shiny-eyed excitement to frustration. Moving in from the fringes to respond to her implicit plea for escape, Tim says: 'Oh, actually, I think Gareth might want to see you' – and they're finally together.

At the party later in the episode, the clandestine glance is again crucial to Tim and Dawn's contact, this time when Lee makes typically insensitive comments about Dawn's aspirations to be an illustrator ('to make money out of it you've got to be good'). Zooming in for a close-up two-shot of Tim and Dawn that lasts almost ten seconds, we see Dawn shoot Lee a dirty look as Tim considers whether to challenge him; Dawn looks down just as Tim shoots a quick, questioning look in her direction

94

The look of love (Christmas Special, Part Two)

before turning back; then, staring ahead, Tim misses the glance she sends him as she looks up. Meanwhile the party DJ plays 'The Look of Love'. The awkwardness doesn't cast a pall over the rest of the evening, however; they get on so well that they avoid eye contact as she prepares to leave; Tim remains stiff, uncertain whether he could bear a peck on the cheek or even to stay in touch; when Dawn hugs him his deadpan face barely conceals his yearning. As she walks away, we and Tim watch her go for a full twenty seconds as Take That's 'Back for Good' winds down. When she's out of sight, he turns to the camera as if to a friend and shrugs his brow in resignation.

The romance seems over, but later, as Yazoo's 'Only You' plays, Dawn comes back into the room. At first we don't notice her, and she doesn't see Tim; she spots him just before the camera sees her and zooms in as she advances across the room to tap him on the shoulder. He turns and after his initial confusion, their eyes lock for the first time in unwary, unself-conscious recognition of what they've fumbled around for so long. Their kiss is gentle, nudging, tender and loaded with

95

Their eyes lock

the suppressed expectation of seven hours' viewing and years of self-policing. Carefully, seriously, as if holding something fragile and invaluable for the first time, he places a hand on her cheek, her throat, indifferent at last to the look of the lens and those around them. They lock hands, turn their backs on the camera and walk from the room.

Comedy about television

The characters of *The Office*, then, are marked out by their acute awareness of the camera. Sometimes this has no discernible effect on them; often it produces a heightened self-consciousness that subtly modifies their behaviour in the hope of regulating their image for public broadcast; and at its most pronounced, it results in words and actions that wouldn't have happened without the camera's presence. Expanding a programme's subject matter to include its own production process inevitably depends on a high degree of audience sophistication; viewers must be sufficiently media savvy to spot the gaps in the characters' self-presentation, to look through their eyes and see the camera looking back. Encouraged by the multiple registers of docusoap this mode had been increasingly exploited by British comedy shows of the 1990s, which capitalised on the audience knowingness about media production that became one of the decade's cultural hallmarks; just as factual programming had been advancing into mainstream light entertainment territory, comedians had been making play with the formal apparatus of documentary and reportage and the opportunities for embarrassment afforded by the misguided assumption of control of the camera. The achievement of *The Office* was to marry these two strands, offering both the emotional effect associated with documentary style and the sophisticated postmodern humour of camera play: it was through Brent's cack-handed attempts at self-promotion that we learned to understand his character.

British comedy has long attended to the fractious potential of the relation between subject and camera, notably through the trope of the vox pop: a dragged-up Dick Emery would send an interviewer flying with a well-placed shove; a well-intentioned anorak-clad geek could clumsily smear grease on the lens in *A Bit of Fry and Laurie* (1989–95). Such jokes aped the form of conventional reportage but retained its implicit superiority over its everyday subjects: such characters don't 'get' television and inadvertently disrupt its operation through incompetence; any effort made to exert 'ownership' of the camera in such set-ups leads to embarrassment because of their status as outsiders to the media. In the 90s, however, this approach was expanded – or inverted – to take advantage of those whose very living was predicated on such ownership: celebrities. Caroline Aherne's *Mrs Merton Show* (BBC2, 1995–8) followed Dame Edna Everage in exploiting a larger-than-life persona to ask cheeky questions of famous guests, without crossing the line into outright confrontation. When Paul Kaye's character 'Dennis Pennis' started conducting guerrilla interviews (initially for *The Sunday Show*, BBC2, 1995) at showbiz events, the notion that an unknown performer could use the simple presence of established public figures as the butt of his humour still had a novel tang. Using the universally recognised credential of being 'from the BBC' as bait, Pennis attracted celebrities who expected an opportunity for self-promotion but found they were in fact lined up for insult. (He asked Demi Moore whether she'd consider keeping her clothes on in a film and Steve Martin why he wasn't funny any more.) The success of such gags stemmed from the disruption of their victims' assumptions about the power hierarchy at work: the frisson lay not just in seeing a star turned into a gull, but in witnessing their often genuine anger that the power of the lens could be used against them. This rug-pulling element made them 'prank' comedy, but of a kind quite distinct from such series as *Candid Camera* (1976), *Beadle's About* (1986–96) or, latterly, *Trigger Happy TV* (2000–1), all of which played tricks on members of the public, or even such celebrity-based equivalents as the 'Gotcha Oscars' on *Noel's House Party* (1993). Where those went to great lengths to conceal their recording equipment – indeed, generated suspense from the possibility of its being discovered – Pennis's encounters retained as their *sine qua non* the explicit presence of the camera: here it was the very desire to be filmed that made the gulls vulnerable.

The most accomplished exploitation of this dynamic was found in Chris Morris's *Brass Eye* (Channel 4, 1997, followed by a one-off special on paedophilia in 2001). Having established with the ludicrous vox pops of *The Day Today* (BBC2, 1994) that members of the public would spout nonsense if placed in front of a camera and asked to do so, Morris pulled off the more sensational coup of enlisting the support of celebrities and public figures for a series of preposterous campaigns. At their simplest these stings comprised studio-based interviews in which Morris embarked upon a subject which did not bear logical examination (or indeed was patent nonsense) to test how long his guest would persist in discussing it with apparent sincerity. In the more complex set-ups, participants were invited by a bogus pressure group to campaign against such fictitious outrages as the drug 'cake' or the perils of 'heavy electricity' by reading scripts to camera, purportedly for inclusion in information videos which, they were told, might be shown on television. Like Pennis's victims, Morris's willingly approached the camera with the assumption of mastery (although unlike them, most of Morris's subjects didn't even realise they had been duped until long after their participation). The mere fact of being filmed seemed to offer sufficient reassurance of the legitimacy of the causes espoused; it was only when the full context was revealed with transmission that alarm bells sounded. Thoughtlessly confident that the alchemy of the lens would automatically confer credibility on them, Morris's gulls volunteered to perform laughable actions not despite the camera's presence but because of it. Much of the humour came from the gulf between their sophisticated knowledge of media processes and the sheer inanity of the subject matter to which it was applied, the subjects' complacency evident in shifts in register – from business-like indifference to po-faced cod-concern – corresponding to whether or not they thought they were being recorded for transmission. Here's the illusionist Paul Daniels shooting an appeal on behalf of an imaginary East German elephant with her trunk lodged in her anus:

'Come on – help us get that trunk out.' Paul Daniels in *Brass Eye*

99

> I'll give you another one that you can cut in later. I'll just say that and
> you can cut it in later – go to the elephant, go to somewhere else. And –
> All right? Still rolling? [Pauses, adopts grave expression, points to
> camera] Come on – help us get that trunk out.

There's not much difference between this and Brent's suggestion of
running a Comic Relief phone number across the screen, a similar
mismatch between the attention paid to the form of the contribution
and its substance. To be recorded is more important than to offer
anything worthy of record.

Brass Eye drew attention to the regrettable eagerness of both
entertainers and politicians to appear on camera holding forth about

and even agitating for action over non-existent issues. At his best, Sacha Baron Cohen's character Ali G demonstrated a similar point. First appearing on Channel 4's *The 11 O'Clock Show* in 1998 (the show that would give Gervais widespread exposure two years later), Ali, like Pennis, was the stand-out contributor to an otherwise patchy show who achieved popularity through an interview persona that exposed his unwitting subjects to ridicule. But where Pennis simply used celebrities as butts to his wisecracks, Ali's post-*Brass Eye* approach was more complex: posing as 'the voice of youth', the primary source of humour was Ali's own ignorance and prejudice, but its most unsettling effect was to reveal the willingness of many of his guests to indulge or even egg on his small-mindedness. This seemed to be motivated either by fear of appearing uncool – with the presence of the camera again prompting concern for the appearance of credibility rather than its substance – or by Ali's ostensible encouragement of an environment in which politically incorrect sentiments were legitimised, rather as Louis Theroux's faux-naïve interview technique could elicit unexpectedly revealing comments from profile subjects who let their guard down.

100

If the cod-interview revealed how the fact of being filmed could supplant basic common sense, another development in TV comedy form exploited effects resulting from a documentary shooting style. Comedians had previously produced parodies of documentary formats, both as sketches within such series as *Victoria Wood As Seen on TV* (BBC2, 1985–7) and *French and Saunders* (BBC2, 1987–) and as entire programmes, such as the investigative journalism spoof *This Is David Lander* (Channel 4, 1988). The fly-on-the-wall was sufficiently popular by 1994 for *The Day Today* to run several deadpan institution-based spoofs (including one titled 'The Office'), while the success of the fully fledged docusoap led to sustained take-offs of the format, with both *Operation Good Guys* (BBC2, 1997–2000), about a police squad, and *Boyz Unlimited* (Channel 4, 1999), about a fledgling boy-band, basing jokes around their larger-than-life characters' awareness of their status as filmed subjects with prospective showbiz careers; *Good Guys* even featured senior BBC figures like Head of Entertainment Paul

Jackson. There was also accomplished mockery of more conventional institution-based observational documentary in *People Like Us*, which transferred from Radio 4 to BBC2 in 1999, while the fly-on-the-wall relationship portraits of *Human Remains* (BBC2, 2000) used documentary techniques to showcase their almost indecently fully realised characters.

The 1990s also saw the vérité aesthetic of hand-held cameras, imperfect framing and variable sound quality beginning to find application to comedy programming beyond explicit genre pastiche. This stylistic crossover is more often associated with drama – in America, emergency-based serials such as *NYPD Blue* (1993–2005) and *ER* (1994–) used it to ape the adrenalised immediacy of reality series like *Cops*; in the UK, Tony Garnett applied it to the everyday concerns of *This Life* (1996–7) as well as his own drama *The Cops* (1998–2001) – but the approach was arguably first applied to situation comedy. Based around the neurotic self-absorption of a late-night talk-show host, *The Larry Sanders Show* (HBO, 1992) was divided between slick video for the 'broadcast' segments and raw hand-held film stock for the backstage back-stabbings, the tenor shifting correspondingly from jovial, high-gloss mainstream patter to scenes characterised by strong language, naturalistic performances and no laugh track. As *Brass Eye* would later, the series made play with the gulf between 'on' and 'off'.

Arguably the first British comedy to adopt this faux-documentary style was also about an egocentric chat-show host pre-occupied with the state of his career. Alan Partridge had been created as sports reporter for the Radio 4 news parody *On the Hour* (1990) and fleshed out in his own radio chat show, *Knowing Me, Knowing You* (1993), first broadcast in the same year as *Larry Sanders*' debut. It was followed by a cod behind-the-scenes programme, *Knowing Knowing Me, Knowing You* (1993), which made explicit the gulf between Partridge's 'on' and 'off' personae (not that it had been the most efficiently patrolled border – indeed, its frequent breaching was one of the running jokes of the initial series). Both radio series transferred to

BBC2 in 1994 (*On the Hour* becoming *The Day Today*). *Knowing Me, Knowing You . . . with Alan Partridge* was both sharp-eyed genre spoof and relishable character vehicle, with particular attention paid to Partridge's obsession with his own status within the C-list light-entertainment food chain and his concern for contractual niceties, budget decisions and set design. Partridge faced calamity when he accidentally killed a guest in his final show; ostensibly given a second chance in the shape of a Christmas special, he botched this too by punching a fictitious senior BBC commissioner called Tony Hayers. Both crises provided the opportunity for some nicely judged formal slippage, when the chat-show format gave way to an accomplished approximation of the suspenseful frisson associated with live TV gone wrong – wheeling cameras, a flash of an ident card, visibly confused crew members. In these liminal moments we glimpsed Partridge paralysed with panic, no longer the smug master of the camera but a man in desperate limbo.

His TV career over, the character nevertheless resurfaced in *I'm Alan Partridge* (BBC2, 1997), a fly-on-the-wall sitcom following Partridge's post-chat life. Downplaying quick-fire one-liners, fixed studio sets and self-contained farce plotting, the series was built around nuanced character observation, hand-held camerawork, significant portions of location shooting and looser stories which reflected Partridge's aimless existence yet also had a degree of continuity across the series. Much of this was closer to docusoap than conventional sitcom; indeed, had Steve Coogan and Armando Iannucci decided to go the whole hog and allowed their characters to show awareness of the camera's presence (as did the subjects of the spoof video diaries created in 1994 for Coogan's characters Paul and Pauline Calf) and present the series as an *Osbournes*-style observational format with Partridge playing up to a TV crew following his post-chat career, *I'm Alan Partridge* would have pre-empted even more of *The Office*'s formal effects. (According to Gupta, the creators of both characters were aware of the crossover: 'On the first series [of *The Office*] Stephen would constantly shout at Ricky: "Too Partridge! You've gone too Partridge!"

But then the flipside of that was being at the Comedy Awards after the first series and being collared by Coogan, who was in slightly verbose form, if you know what I mean, and he kept saying: "When we did the last series of *Partridge* I was just worried about doing Brent, I didn't want to do Brent."') In the event *I'm Alan Partridge* retained a laugh track and a central character who, however sophisticatedly drawn, probably remained too large to be considered naturalistic, even if those around him could be.

Though it wasn't trying to pass as docusoap *per se*, the series was still concerned with television as subject matter: just as *Larry Sanders*' double register contrasted on-screen slickness with behind-the-scenes rancour, *I'm Alan Partridge*'s documentary aesthetic provided a telling contrast with the glamorously over-designed milieu of celebrity chat from which the character was now exiled. There he had been able to appeal (however misguidedly) to his claim over the camera as proof against challenge; like *Brass Eye*'s victims, and David Brent, his self-worth had been located in the fact of being filmed. Indeed, the vain and careerist preoccupation with being on television was what provided the consistent throughline to Partridge's career: his wheedling attempts to get from radio to TV and then to engineer the commissioning of a second TV series were a running joke; it's no coincidence that the fictional commissioning editor Hayers was the only supporting character to appear in both radio and TV series of *Knowing Me, Knowing You* and *I'm Alan Partridge*, of which one comic highlight was a meeting in which Alan served up a litany of inane programme pitches ('*Monkey Tennis*?').

I'm Alan Partridge was only the first of a number of British series to put the vérité look to comic effect. Caroline Aherne's *The Royle Family* moved even further away from the traditional sitcom model, offering no laugh track and a melancholic pop song for a theme tune as well as slow-paced narrative that built across the series and the accretion of highly naturalistic character through minor incident, including unresolved emotional flare-ups. The often static camera and highly limited setting (we seldom leave the family's front room and never the house) resulted in an unusual intimacy and a high level of audience association. Again, television itself was of central importance: the camera was usually located in the position of the TV set, at the centre of attention, and some episodes consisted of no more than the family of couch potatoes bantering in front of the box as the camera drifted from one to the other. Never had the form of a programme so closely resembled the circumstances of its consumption.

Aherne's follow-up to *The Royle Family*, *Dossa and Joe* (BBC2, 2002), was set across a broader, less-closeted setting more fitting to its Australian location, but it retained *The Royle Family*'s naturalistic attention to familial and social dynamics. (*Sylvania Waters* seemed to be a touchstone here, as for the Australian series *Kath and Kim*, which debuted in 2001.) In addition, Dossa and Joe's sessions with an off-screen counsellor cultivated an almost talking-head feel, as if they were confiding in the audience itself. (*This Life* used exactly the same tactic; the 'diary rooms' of reality game shows fulfil a similar function.) The emotional impact of *Marion and Geoff* (BBC2, 2000) was achieved through the unguarded intimacy of its video-diary format, with considerable pathos resulting from the dramatically ironic discrepancy between the unfailingly chipper attitude of Keith (Rob Brydon) and the grim reality of his life as he describes it to a dashboard-mounted camera, which he considerately disables if he feels it might be threatening someone else's privacy.

104

The Office, then, fits neatly alongside British television comedies of its time in assuming audiences' familiarity with the circumstances of TV production and consumption, and exploiting such knowingness both for the purposes of humour and within its formal fabric. But no other programme had combined mistaken claims of camera ownership, the tension between behaviour 'on' and 'off', plausible genre pastiche and an emotionally affecting naturalistic mode to such effect. It's worth noting, however, that Gervais and Merchant claim never to have considered their work in this context. 'People always accuse us of ripping off the wrong things,' Merchant complains. 'Yeah,' Gervais agrees, 'we didn't rip those off, we ripped off American stuff. I don't think there's a British sitcom in there, from my point of view.' Merchant says that

> People talk about *The Royle Family* and us suddenly doing this new low-key vérité style, but it's been around for years. Maybe it's a new thing on television but that speaks more about television than about our being out in the forefront. There's not really anything that we're doing that someone like Woody Allen hasn't done – overlapping dialogue and low-key chat – or *Diner*, three or four people start talking. It's not a new thing at all, it's just people haven't seen it on television or applied to a sitcom maybe, or previously it's not been considered worthy of that much effort perhaps.

As we have seen, a preoccupation with the processes of production has been characteristic of Gervais and Merchant's other TV work, particularly *Meet Ricky Gervais*, with its conspicuously shoddy title sequence, discussion of programme priorities and inclusion of 'behind the scenes' material. It is also evident in the series they made after *The Office*, *Extras* (BBC2, 2005). Featuring Gervais as Andy Millman, a 'background artist' constantly angling for even one line in one of the film or TV productions in which he appears, it again shows a fascination with the lure of the lens and the gap between 'on' and 'off', with the casting of major celebrities (such as Ben Stiller, Kate Winslet and Samuel L. Jackson) as tongue-in-cheek versions of themselves adding further layers of ambiguity.

105

The uses of comedy

The Office's engagement with television as subject matter is also illustrated by the extent to which David Brent relies on gags and tropes lifted from TV comedians as the basis for his own generally calamitous attempts at humour. Where Partridge's personality was structured around a nexus of signifiers of naff culture (Wagon Wheels, Vangelis, World of Leather), Brent's depends on his co-option of comedy: in I.i alone he tries to raise laughs through reference to *The Darling Buds of May* (1991–3), *EastEnders*, Vic Reeves and Bob Mortimer and adverts for Resolve, Levi's and Budweiser, not to mention the off-the-shelf humour of the wall-mounted 'Big Mouth Billy Bass' ('You can't put a price on comedy'). The rest of the series is littered with such references, often to decidedly stale stock sources of humour, often immediately followed by an explanation to ensure the reference is recognised (' "You can't beat a bit of bully!" *Bullseye*'). Brent's clear hope is to be thought of as funny simply through association with things he finds funny, as if merely pointing at a stuffed ITV Digital toy with a gawpy grin were enough to qualify for the status of comedian: '"Monkey!" ' he grunts in imitation of Johnny Vegas's ads for the network. 'That's an example of the laughs we have here.' As Gervais says, 'Brent was a man who would stand in a bar and shout *Fast Show* characters 'cause it was easier than thinking of his own jokes.'

It's an approach *The Fast Show* (1994–7) itself parodied with its cringeworthy office comedian character, Colin Hunt, who regales his colleagues with gags and catchphrases lifted from the previous night's telly.

Monkey! (II.i)

For obvious reasons, Colin was one of the series' few characters who didn't have his own catchphrase; for the same reasons, *The Office* offered no real catchphrases of its own. There were certainly repeated linguistic tropes, mostly centred around Brent: his preening responses to non-existent enquiries ('What, her? Just writing an article on me'); his attempts to suggest a point has been made through use of the dangling 'so' and a pregnant pause (*The Little Book of Calm* he brandishes at the motivational speaking event in II.iv has a 'foreword by Duncan Goodhew, so –'); the non-committal phrase 'in a way'; the deflection of his own crassness by claiming to observe regrettable behaviour by someone else ('That's a shame') or in general ('which I hate'). These last few come closest to quotable catchphrases, but require an original set-up each time rather than being easily repeatable. Yet once a show becomes widely popular, fans – and journalists – like to home in on a phrase that immediately identifies a show, providing a sense of common ownership. Gervais suggests that 'I said "fact" once in one episode [II.i] and it became a catchphrase. I mean, that's a desperate nation that needs a catchphrase!' Brent's dance from II.v also rapidly acquired something like catchphrase currency, giving fans something they could at least try to replicate down the pub – and eventually chant for Gervais to perform when he appeared on stage for the London Live 8 concert in July 2005. As Gupta says, 'Suddenly people had something they could all do. Before that you could just go: "Did you see it?" "Yeah, did you see it?" "Wasn't it good?" ' Atalla also recalls noting when the show's popularity reached that critical level: 'We were somehow getting into the territory of catchphrase comedy, like people quoting Harry Enfield down the pub, despite not having catchphrases.'

107

The character of Brent does, however, believe he has catchphrases, as befits his misguidedly self-appointed status as a professional comedian ('There's a weight of intellect behind my comedy,' he claims in I.ii). After working himself up into near-hysterics in I.iii with a prop-based improv session using the giant inflatable penis given to Tim as a birthday present, Brent suddenly turns bitterly serious when he senses a possible threat to his position.

Brent: Remember, you're only as old as the woman you feel.

Gareth: I say that sometimes.

Brent: Yeah, I heard you say it the other day, and I thought, 'He's using one of my catchphrases'. I don't mind influencing a younger comedian – you're not a comedian – but, you know, I usually credit someone if I use their comedy.

Later, in II.i, Brent gives a more equivocally charitable response to one of Gareth's attempts at humour, saying 'That's the sort of stuff I write. I mean, you didn't write it, you just told it, but, you know – Well done.' The role-playing exercises of I.iv's training day offer a further platform for Brent's acting and musical pretensions while the second series provides a string of set-piece opportunities for Brent to map his supposed talents as entertainer onto work-related events: the motivational speech in II.iv, that astonishing dance routine in II.v and, most saliently, the welcome speech Brent gives to the new arrivals from Slough in II.i, which he explicitly frames as a 'lunchtime gig' whose humiliating collapse can be blamed on his new nemesis Neil ('Often an amateur will stitch up a professional'). Gervais and Merchant slightly stack the cards against Brent here, having the staff greet with disproportionate warmth the equally mediocre jokes Neil tells before Brent's address. The comparison does, however, underline the fact that making an audience laugh depends on amiability and charisma as much as material *per se*. Brent evinces neither of these during his disastrous sally: clutching a thick sheaf of notes he tries to palm off on his audience a collection of second-hand gags, responding with surprise, embarrassing self-awareness and growing resentment to their continued silence ('Get to the real stuff . . . there's better ones than that . . . That's the Two Ronnies! Do you not like that? That is classic stuff!'). Eventually his desperation leads him into an awkwardly multilayered impression of a figure from the paper industry imagined in *Fawlty Towers* Nazi walk mode: Ricky Gervais playing David Brent imitating Eric Hitchmough as John Cleese playing Basil Fawlty impersonating

108

Adolf Hitler. Not funny, but the ultimate illustration of Brent's confusion of reference with wit. With a last throw of the dice he attempts a straightforward catchphrase rip-off, his ultimate failure signalled by a mortifying rictus and deflated lobbing in of the towel: 'Has everyone heard of Harry Enfield? *Has everyone heard of Harry Enfield?* Yes. Right then, okay. Then who's this? "I do not believe you wanted to do that. Only me!" Oh, come on! Aah, you try something and . . .'

That coercive tone flares again and again when Brent feels under-appreciated: in II.ii, determined to have the Swindon intake acknowledge that his office environment is more relaxed than Neil's, he barks 'Say "yes", then, if you think it's more laid-back!' The problem here is Brent's location of so much self-worth in a field for which he has no aptitude, resulting in the unwinnable situation of instructing people to find him funny. 'Chill out, yeah?' he commands in the last scene of II.i. 'Trust me, this is what I do, all right? You will never work in a place like this again. This is brilliant – fact. Yeah? And you'll never have another boss like me – someone who's basically a chilled-out entertainer.' That he is neither chilled-out nor entertaining guarantees their failure to subscribe to this. Their belief that Neil's Swindon branch was 'more of a laugh' rubs it in, prompting Brent's pitiful appeals to Dawn to shore up his flagging confidence in II.ii.

109

Brent: Do you think Neil's funny?

Dawn: Do I think Neil's funny? Er –

Brent: Yeah.

Dawn: I don't really know him, David.

Brent: But he's not funnier than me?

Dawn: No, definitely not.

Brent: No. Right. I wish you'd tell that to the Swindon lot – miserable bunch of – Ain't they? Some of them. Boring.

Dawn: Mmm.

Brent: What's your favourite stuff that I do, comedy-wise?

Dawn: Um – Oh, there's too much.

Brent: Impressions?

Dawn: Oh, yes . . .

The single most squirm-inducing instance of such attempted coercion comes with Brent's motivational speech in II.iv, when he bypasses humour altogether and simply tells his audience to laugh along with him, embarking on a snowballing crescendo of hoots and howls that only widens the distance between him and his audience the longer it goes on. Such stony-faced silence is of course utterly typical of responses to his 'material'; his conception of himself as a professional comedian is possible only by virtue of the colossal blind spot he has when it comes to his jokes and the response they elicit. 'They're cracking up,' he says of Tim and Dawn in I.iii, who aren't; 'They seemed to go for it, eh?' is his equally deluded response to the motivational speech in II.iv. The pattern is established from the off, with the slew of rotten gags that punctuate the opening minutes of I.i (the unfortunate question 'Elaine left you yet?'; the crass mention of 'the crack of Dawn'; the use of the 'special filing cabinet' that rebounds on him when Jennifer arrives).

These misfirings also neatly illustrate the negative impact Brent's attempts at humour tend to reap: embarrassment for himself, rankling resentment from his staff, increasingly wearisome disdain from his superiors. At best his botched humour results in pained silences, rendered all the more acute by the lack of a laugh track. But it's a short hop from dampening the mood to causing genuine offence. In II.i, complaints are lodged against Brent's racist gags while in the first Christmas Special, his ill-humoured reaction to his own botching even of facile *Blind Date*-style one-liners results in ugly confrontation with the nightclub audience on whom he is meant to be impressing his status as entertainer. In II.v, he manages to reduce one of Gareth's friends (played by Merchant, who is very tall) to tears through attempted banter:

Brent: Oh, bloody hell. What's the weather like up there?

Oggy: Oh, I've heard that before.

Brent: Parents put you in a grow bag when you were little, did they?

Oggy: That's an old one.

Brent: 'Let's grow ourselves a big, lanky, goggle-eyed freak of a son.'

Oggy: All right, calm down, mate. There's no need to be offensive.

The small distance between supposed communal laughter and aggressive peer pressure is repeatedly shown: when Gareth (in his first ever appearance) hoves into view honking 'Wassssuup' as he whacks Tim round the head with a newspaper (I.i), he is using a joke as a fig-leaf for the expression of playground violence; Lee's restraint of Tim while the others remove his shoes and lob them over the roof (I.iii) offers a further discomfiting instance of group laughter at the expense of a scapegoat. Comic Relief Day (II.v) provides a unique context in which those who resent the imposition of such humour – even in as aggressive a form as the stripping of a struggling employee – can be accused of being not just killjoys but uncharitable to boot. There are moments when Brent himself is made the object of aggressive laughter, through being forced to recount an instance of his own inanity: after the quiz in I.iii, Finch makes him tell everyone who he thought the Cuban revolutionary leader was ('Fray Bentos'); in II.vi, Neil makes him recite to Jennifer the game-show pitch he has been working on instead of a Wernham Hogg report; and in the first Christmas Special, Gareth – in an index of his new power – makes Brent tell the camera about his failed single. In these instances, pressured into presenting himself as an object of ridicule, Brent in fact becomes pitiful, even sympathetic.

All in the name of fun: Comic Relief Day (II.v)

Brent claims that 'There are limits to my comedy. There are things that I will never laugh at, like the handicapped, because there's nothing funny about them.' For Merchant and Gervais, however – especially the latter, if his other work is any indication – risqué topics such as disability, sexuality and race are eagerly exploited in order to mine uncomfortable humour from Brent's cack-handed attempts to negotiate them without causing offence. His inane lip service against sexism is particularly excruciating, with his attitude to his ward Donna demonstrating a chauvinistic double standard by which jokes can be made at the expense of other girls but not the one he sees as his 'property': in a rare instance of Brent rejecting humour he expels an employee from a meeting for making one too many jokes about Donna's attractiveness (I.ii); two episodes later his sycophantic giggling at Finchy's innuendoes stalls when he realises is the subject Donna ('No, don't – do it to other girls, that's fine'). The introduction in series two of one mixed-race character and another who uses a wheelchair provides even more plentiful opportunities for Brent to fail to conceal his unreconstructed ignorance.

In fact the only thing Brent won't laugh at is himself. The humour he professes to encourage throughout his office is in fact seen to be an indicator of rank, to be applied from the top down rather than bottom up: he responds with extreme prickliness when Dawn joins in good-naturedly with his own banter about his drinking in I.i ('How many pints have I drunk this week, if you're counting?'), or when in II.iv he inadvertently prompts Gareth to reveal that 'A lot of people are laughing at the heels on your shoes' and calling him nicknames. Despite his protestations that 'Porno laughs are not funny' it's clear that Brent's anger at the joke email in I.ii stems from the use of his own image, digitally imposed onto a pornographic photo, as a source of humour to all the other employees. When, following Brent's accusation of Tim as the result of Gareth's investigation, the picture's true provenance is uncovered, Brent finds his hypocritical approach short-circuited:

Tim: Whoa, whoa, whoa. Columbo here figured it out, did he? Well, 113 yeah, of course, gee, sorry. Yeah, I must be guilty if you've got your best man on the case.

Brent: Stop trying to be funny for one second, Tim, okay, and listen, okay? . . . You're taking the piss and I'm getting f–ing sick of it.

Tim: David, it wasn't me, okay? It was your good friend Chris Finch. He used my computer. He said he was your best mate and you'd find it hilarious.

Brent: Oh, er – No, it is. That was never in question. I think it's bloody hilarious . . .

Malcolm: So it's not offensive now it's Chris Finch?

Brent: Let's not dwell on whether it is or isn't this or – Let's stop degrading women, shall we, please? Let's have a laugh with them, not at them. Let's have a laugh at work, with women, at us, if anything.

Brent's slapping down of Tim's 'trying to be funny' shows his determination here, given how easy it usually is to get him on side through the use of humour (in the first episode we see Tim secure Brent's sympathy over embedding Gareth's stapler in jelly by quipping 'It's only a trifling matter'). Here, however, Brent finds himself in an impossible situation. Finchy is the one person he is willing to be ridiculed by, placing more stock in association with what Brent perceives to be Finch's superior sense of humour ('funny *and* clever') than he does in his own vanity, let alone his half-cocked feminist gestures (though he is at least aware of the conflict, constantly trying to explain away Finch's offensiveness to the camera – 'Close to the bone but harmless, innit?'). Brent perceives their relationship as that of a professional comedy double act:

> We're like Morecambe and Wise when we get together. Actually, not Morecambe and Wise, 'cause there's no dead wood, so – I'm more sort of character-based and he's more of a gag man. I do gags as well, but I mean – Good together, you know, by now. (I.iii)

114

Caught in the middle: Brent unwilling to laugh at Neil's jokes (II.iii)

It's clear from their interaction, however, that Finch is a bully, using Brent as the butt of corny gags in an attempt to enhance his own prestige. The rapport quickly turns sour if he feels Brent has become a handicap – as when their team (named the 'Dead Parrots' in tribute to their shared passion for second-hand humour) loses the quiz in I.iii.

> **Finch:** I'll write the questions next time and you can have this fat bastard on your side.
>
> **Brent:** Banter.
>
> **Finch:** No, it's not banter.
>
> **Brent:** It's not banter. Not now.

Such treatment does nothing to dampen Brent's shameless sycophancy – he provides for Finch the type of indiscriminately appreciative audience that he himself clearly craves – though it comes in for a more substantial challenge in the second series when Finch is allied with Brent's nemesis Neil, whose smooth efficacy largely functions to throw Brent's bumbling into sympathetic relief. Having made a point of rejecting Neil's humour as worthless, Brent is stymied when Finchy proves to be an admirer, even admitting to stealing Neil's jokes: 'I do not nick 'em, I borrow 'em,' he says when they meet in II.iii. Brent is left trying to establish a pecking order by dishing out praise and opprobrium for more or less identical comments (about an unseen former employee, now unemployed), with neither of his interlocutors remotely interested in his opinions:

> **Finch:** Tell her I'll take her up the dole office.
>
> **Neil:** The 'dole orifice'!
>
> **Brent:** Rubbish.
>
> [Finch laughs.]

Finch: Well, I've got a vacancy she can fill.

Brent: That's better. His work. Don't try and –

Finch's gag doesn't actually work, of course, but such jockeying is typical of Brent's conception of humour as a measure of power and status. It's only at the end of the Christmas Specials that he has the necessary confidence for a forthright rejection of Finch's belittling snipes – a confidence apparently resulting from his date Carol's provision of a receptive audience for his humour ('Yeah, he's funny,' she tells the director at the end of the evening).

Humour is equally crucial to the rapport between Tim and Dawn. Tim is about the only character who cracks jokes that make us laugh: his one-liners and practical jokes, unlike Brent's, are actually funny, whether he's tormenting Gareth over his mobile phone or wondering what having 'something for the old people' at the Christmas party would consist of ('Werther's Originals? A phone call from your son?'). Although other characters are amused – 'I don't know why you're laughing,' Gareth sniffs at an employee after Tim drops his stapler out of the window in I.i – it's Dawn who's most closely allied to his wit. Their mutual sympathy is established through jokes, most of them at the reliably humourless Gareth's expense, Dawn watching with glee as Tim torments him or joining Tim as they gigglingly exhibit to the camera Gareth's investigation signs or goad him into gay innuendo under the guise of enquiring about his Territorial Army manoeuvres. They also share a similar line in ironic observation. Compare the talking heads in which Tim describes his birthday present from his mum (a baseball cap with a built-in radio, I.iii) and Dawn recalls how Lee proposed to her (I.iv):

I like ballet, I love the novels of Proust, I love the work of Alain Delon. And that's, I think, what influenced her in buying me HatFM.

He did it in one of the little Valentine's message bits in the paper. I think he had to pay for it by the word, 'cause it just said: 'Lee love Dawn. Marriage, question mark.' Which, you know, I like, 'cause it's not often you get something that's both romantic and thrifty.

It's clear that Dawn and Lee do not share such a bond, with her occasional sarcastic asides irritating him (when he spots them). In I.iii, in response to Lee's statement that theirs 'ain't gonna be a flashy wedding', Dawn mutters 'heaven forbid', before indirectly stoking tension between Lee and Tim:

Lee: You can probably go out and get a little part-time cleaning job or something.

Dawn: Gotta dream the dream.

[Tim laughs.]

Lee: What's that?

Tim: No, I was just laughing at what Dawn said.

Lee: 'Cause you're such a big high-flier, yeah?

Tim: No! I was just – just laughing at her joke, that's all.

Lee: When you start getting a life, mate, you can take the mickey out of ours, all right?

Tim: Lee, I'm not having a go! I'm just, you know – It's just that she made a joke.

When Lee and Dawn row in the following episode, it's Tim's jokes that cheers her up; the suggestion that their shared sense of humour might make Dawn better suited to Tim than to Lee is made explicit in this awkward exchange from II.vi, which starts with Tim reading from a women's magazine and unfolds with Dawn conspicuously avoiding his eye:

Tim: What do you look for in a man?

Dawn: Rugged good looks.

Lee: You always told me it was a good sense of humour.

Dawn: Yeah, you've got that. You've got a good sense of humour.

Lee: Yeah, I know. I know.

Tim and Dawn's estrangement in series two is expressed through the absence of shared jokes, with Tim knocking back Dawn's attempts to share humour – 'You'd have laughed' or 'Do you want to wind up Gareth for a bit?' (His eventual agreement to the latter signals a rapprochement.) The romance between Tim and Rachel that grows throughout the series is also described through humour. Dawn jealously notes Tim making her laugh during the fire drill, while Rachel is notably more proactive than Dawn in instigating pranks, either at Gareth's expense or as a way of Tim proving himself: she dares him to plant a dildo in Brent's office ''cause it'll make me laugh' (II.iii). Comedy becomes the ground on which Rachel and Dawn's rivalry for Tim's affections plays out, with Dawn trying to tempt him to Brent's motivational speech 'for a laugh' (II.iv) and Rachel impressing him by making Gareth unwittingly humiliate himself. In II.iii, Dawn is irritated by Rachel's muscling in on the self-congratulatory glow following a successful prank at Gareth's expense but by II.vi – shortly before Tim dumps her – Rachel is an outsider to the laughter at Gareth's suggestive speakerphone conversation, the framing excluding her from a composition that bonds Tim and Dawn, hinting at a possible union that the end of series two in fact denies.

The Christmas Special makes a point of noting both Tim and Dawn's lack of a playmate: in the first part, new secretary Mel is too dim or officious to join in Tim's mockery of Gareth, while we see Dawn making a couple of sarky gags that Tim would appreciate but Lee ignores. But their shared humour does unite them in the second part: when she visits the office, it's taunting Gareth that breaks the ice

118

between them; at the party, the same effect is achieved by their mutual appreciation of the humiliation of pregnant employee Anne by warehouse foreman Glynn. Later, Lee's disruption of their mockery of Gareth – 'They're winding you up, mate' – visibly disappoints Dawn, presumably contributing to her decision shortly afterwards to leave him for Tim.

These last two instances also illustrate the differences between the white-collar and blue-collar environments. *The Office*'s acknowledgment of the blue-collar sector is unusual in a docusoap context but provides an intriguing glimpse of two cultures rubbing along somewhat uncomfortably. In contrast to recent films with comparable set-ups, *The Office* offers neither simplistic oppositions nor politically charged confrontation: there's none of the wish fulfilment fantasy of Mike Judge's *Office Space* (1999), whose hero ultimately finds satisfaction in quitting his IT job to become a manual worker; nor the agitated engagement of Laurent Cantet's *Les Ressources humaines* (1999), a film about the breakdown in industrial relations that erupts at a factory where a young graduate, whose father works on the shop floor, has just joined the executive fast track. *The Office*'s encounters between blue- and white-collar worlds are uncomfortable but not explosive, ranging from wary to hostile: it's certainly not possible for middle-class viewers to adopt the cosy, patronising attitude to the working-class characters that has arguably been a characteristic of reality programming from *The Family* through to *Driving School* (1997) and *Big Brother* (1999). Granada's Director of Programmes, David Plowright, once suggested that 'You are making programmes in which the working class are showing themselves up, albeit endearingly, so the middle classes can have a chuckle'[28] but in *The Office*, it's more often the blue-collar workers laughing at the white. When Tim takes the newcomers for a tour of the warehouse in II.iii, his pith-helmeted pose is only half-joking:

119

Okay, now guys, we're about to enter a warehouse environment. Now, I must warn you that some of the people in here will be working class, so there may be arse cleavage. So just find a partner, hold hands – don't talk to anyone, though, okay?

Tim's attempt to defuse the tension inside earns him a brace of ribald insults just as Brent and Jennifer's excursion to the warehouse in I.ii had ended with Glynn jovially suggesting that she could have sex with Lee's dog (could there be a blunter proof of the death of deference?). When Glynn offers a similarly strong insult to Anne at the Christmas party ('You think we care as much about your baby as you do?' he snorts when she asks him to stop smoking. 'Just 'cause you let some useless tosser blow his beans up your muff?') it manages to provoke some sympathy for a selfish, tactless character whose just deserts we had been keenly anticipating.

'They're not plagued with this ridiculous PC conscience,' Gervais says of the blue-collar characters. 'He didn't have to hold back when he was talking to her because she annoyed him.' Merchant continues:

The warehouse workers at one remove (Christmas Special, Part Two)

We wanted her to get a slight comeuppance inasmuch as she was convinced that she was the centre of the world and that everything revolved around her and her baby and no one from the middle-class white-collar world – maybe except Finch, who wasn't present in that particular scene – would have been that tactless and that thoughtless because no one can really express themselves. We can bring them in and they can speak, because they don't obey the same rules.

Our last glimpse of the warehouse crew shows them having their own party-within-a-party, playing darts in a smoke-filled room viewed from the other side of the door, still at one remove, engaging in laughter that we suspect might not welcome the camera's intrusion.

Sitcom conventions

The Christmas Specials conclude with a big shared joke, everyone – the white-collar workers, at least – for once chuckling along with David Brent doing one of his impressions off the telly. This comes as a particular relief for a show which, as we have seen, so often ended on a downer; the second series had come to a particularly brutal climax, with none of the last half-dozen scenes offering much in the way of laughs – Tim made his second unsuccessful play for Dawn and Brent was rejected by both the motivational-speaking organisation and Wernham Hogg – leaving characters and audience shell-shocked rather than reassured; the first part of the Christmas Special ended with Brent at an even lower ebb. As researcher Joe Moran has observed,

> Ray Carney suggests that we normally laugh at characters in comedies on the assumption that nothing really awful will happen to them. Brent's decline and fall is a kind of betrayal of this compact between the sitcom and its audience. *The Office* tricks the viewer into letting down

her guard, and laughing at something that turns out to be rather tragic.[29]

Arguably, awful things happen to many sitcom characters on a weekly basis – indeed, their failure to slip their bonds could itself be seen as tragic. *The Fall and Rise of Reginald Perrin* (1976–9), for instance, took frustration with the limitations of unending routine as its very premise: in his yearning to escape predictability itself, Reggie was an archetypal sitcom character undergoing an existential crisis. But *The Office*'s episode endings do offer an unusually stringent denial of relief, a failure of everything to be neatly, cathartically resolved that goes against established sitcom form. Self-contained storytelling has been widely noted as a defining element of sitcom: to Mick Bowes, 'The most characteristic feature of the "classic" situation comedy is … circular narrative closure [which] allows little room for progression, making situation comedy radically distinct from soap opera as a form.'[30] Other researchers have discussed the necessary reaffirmation of the continuing situation at each story's conclusion, even suggesting that the primary pleasure of the form is rooted in the fact that nothing ever changes.[31] A sitcom as sophisticated as *The Simpsons* (1989–) can even comment on this, as when Lisa counsels her brother:

> Don't worry, Bart. It seems like every week something odd happens to the Simpsons. My advice is to ride it out, make the occasional smart-alec quip and by next week we'll be back to where we started from, ready for another wacky adventure.[32]

Some sitcoms do offer radical narrative disruptions – the *Blackadder* cycle (1983–9) and *One Foot in the Grave* (1990–6), for instance, ended with the deaths of their lead characters – but these by definition were one-off events made possible only by the shows' termination. *The Office*, however, offers plots that develop over the series: the threat of branch closure in the first run, the arrival of Neil and threat to Brent's job in the second and the will-they-won't-they romantic story with Dawn and Tim throughout. Merchant says

> My big influences are American sitcoms, which have had narrative in them for years, and have had a moving forward trajectory since, particularly *Roseanne*, before that *M*A*S*H* and [later] *Friends*, obviously. There's a long tradition of it over there, particularly because they do such long series they're sort of obliged to move things on. But as well as that we were big fans of movie structure so we knew we had to defer the moment when Tim and Dawn got together because once you have that I don't think you can carry on. I don't think these things work once that moment of consummation has occurred. But nevertheless I still think we couldn't have tolerated it if the characters hadn't moved on, it would have been interminable – the idea that we just said: 'Right, yet another story where Brent makes a buffoon of himself and fails to realise he's done so.'

123

Narrative development is not unprecedented in sitcoms: long-running series such as *The Likely Lads* (1964–6, 1973–4) or *Only Fools and Horses* (1981–2002) incorporated life changes into the fabric of their continuity while shows like *Butterflies* (1978–83) and *Agony* (1979–81) had more weekly progression than previous sitcoms. More recently, American sitcoms like *Friends* and then *Frasier* founded much of their appeal on long-running soap opera-style romance plots of precisely the kind supposedly ruled out by conventional definitions of the form; *Larry Sanders* too had a degree of seriality. The trend has continued since *The Office*, with British series such as *Peep Show* (2003–4), *The Worst Week of My Life* (2004) and Chris Morris's *Nathan Barley* (2005) structured around continuing plots.

Where *The Office* was perhaps more unusual was in its conception from the start as a contained narrative. Where conventional sitcoms were careful to maintain the continuity and sustainability of their setting and characters, *The Office* was always intended to end in a different place from its beginning. It was therefore able to exert an unusually strong narrative pull on its audiences – crucial, Jon Plowman thinks, to its appeal:

> In a multichannel world it's quite difficult to get an audience back week after week after week, particularly to a new thing. The way that Ricky and Stephen did it – particularly in the second series and the last two Specials – was to build in narrative, so you wanted to come back and spend some more time with these characters and see what they were going to do.

Certainly, the degree of narrative anticipation that preceded the Specials was unusual by sitcom standards. Even so, the end of the Specials in fact offers a very conventional kind of reassurance, offering a restoration, however temporary, of 'the good old days' – 'the old gang', as Brent puts it – albeit in an unprecedentedly affectionate key.

The flipside of the circular plot is that the sitcom setting becomes a 'trap' – a well-established genre trope to which *The Office* fully conforms, with Tim and Dawn increasingly enervated by their workplace and Brent increasingly setting his sights on a showbiz career. The idea of sitcom-as-trap is best expounded by Steve Neale and Frank Krutnik, who note of *Steptoe and Son* (1962–74), for instance, that

> most episodes tend to centre upon an attempt by Harold to escape from his frustrating circumstances . . . and his inevitable failure to do so. At the end, each episode restores the situation to 'normal', at the cost of Harold's continuing frustration.[33]

Such an approach, Bruce Crowther and Mike Pinfold add, has an inevitable resonance with those labouring under the kind of bonds that

condemn 'thousands of lives to quiet desperation from which escape is
... impossible'.[34] The potential for desperation written into the form
was something Merchant acknowledges as informing his work on *The
Office*:

> The show that I used to think about when we were doing it was
> *Whatever Happened to the Likely Lads?*, particularly the opening
> credits of that show, so melancholy: 'Oh, what happened to you . . .?' I
> seem to remember it as really sad, and it set the mood every week. And
> just the fact that in that show they would just sit for ten minutes in a
> pub and talk about the fact that their lives had not panned out how
> they hoped. And for a sitcom, particularly such a successful one, it was
> much more like a kitchen sink drama – it was such a far cry even from
> something like *Fawlty Towers*, and especially something like *It Ain't
> Half Hot Mum*.

The other strongly conventional element of *The Office* in the
context of British sitcom is Brent's own character, a self-deluding ogre
with lofty but ultimately pathetic aspirations fully in keeping with a
lineage that runs from Anthony Aloysius Hancock and Alf Garnett
through Captain Mainwaring and Basil Fawlty to Alan Partridge. Like
all such characters, Brent has a blind spot that prevents him realising the
mismatch between his aspirations and his abilities: in his case the
ravenous desire to monopolise attention despite lacking anything like
the talent to merit it. The nadir of his resultant behaviour is surely the
dance from II.v, the Comic Relief episode, spurred by Brent's
unbounded jealousy at Neil's stealing the limelight on what Brent
considers 'his' day. The funny dance is hardly unprecedented in TV
comedy; Elaine in *Seinfeld*, one of Gervais and Merchant's favourite
shows, had a particularly naff routine that she aired at an office party,
losing the respect of her staff.[35] The humour there came from Elaine's
unself-conscious ignorance of the impact her moves made; dancing was

125

The dance (II.v)

an activity she enjoyed, not one in which she took especial pride. While Brent's routine is funny in itself, it takes on its car-crash compulsion because of the gulf between the ferocious conviction of brilliance burning in his eyes and the befuddlement and slight fear creeping over the faces of his spectators – spectators whose attention he demands by wagging a finger around the room as he powers up, upper teeth firmly clamped over his lower lip as he grunts the opening bars of 'Disco Inferno' – a song whose hellish title has surely never found more apt application. Then, legs bowed and arms spinning at the elbow, he squats and jives like some kind of disco hobgoblin, either possessed or constipated. Pointing at the camera as he concludes confirms the horrible group responsibility into which we viewers have been coerced along with those in the room.

The Christmas Specials, with their pop video and personal appearances played off against Brent's continued and unwelcome presence on the Wernham Hogg site, offer a similar clash of registers and demonstrate that – like most ogres – Brent is in fact unable to function outside his comfortable little trap. But it's also in the Christmas Specials that we see the major difference between Brent and other ogres: he has been obliged to confront the discrepancy between his and others' views of himself in a way that his sitcom predecessors weren't. It's an experience familiar to participants in such early reality shows as *The Family* and *The Living Soap* (BBC2, 1993) – both of whose later episodes were partly concerned with the effects on their subjects of the transmission of the initial shows in the run – or indeed *Big Brother* and the like, but not to Mainwaring or Fawlty. The Christmas Specials chart the resultant crisis in Brent's personality, and the cathartic resolution eventually achieved – a fundamental revision of character more in tune with the filmic narratives Merchant and Gervais claim as their primary influences than conventional sitcom circularity.

Another fundamental aspect of *The Office*'s appeal that remains consistent with classical genre conventions is its realism. Where radio comedy was more amenable to flights of fancy, the television sitcom – which emerged in the late 1950s – was essentially naturalistic, depending on simple, real-life set-ups executed with heightened plotting and characterisation; basic formal realism and psychological plausibility played off against narrative escapism and exaggerated behaviour. At root it was a practical approach, Peter Goddard suggests, 'a readily replicable but infinitely variable formula well adapted to the representative strengths and production requirements of television'.[36] But it also had social implications: Terry Lovell argues that such comedy 'shares the goal of realism "to show things as they really are": in the case of comedy to "show the funny side".'[37] From *Steptoe and Son* to *The Likely Lads* to *Only Fools and Horses*, audiences have built up an emotional rapport with sitcom characters, an association founded in realistic characterisation that has often been laced with intimations of despair. Gregory Koseluk claims that *Steptoe* offered 'a mix of humour and pathos that established new ground rules for sitcoms [based on] grim realism and generous doses of pathos',[38] while Jimmy Perry suggested that 'if you want the real reason for *Dad's Army*'s success, it is because it is based on real situations, with real people who are reacting the way we know they are going to react.'[39]

129

Naturalism had arguably died down as a driving force in British sitcom since the rise of alternative comedy: although there were still mainstream mainstays like *Fools and Horses* and newcomers like *Desmonds* (Channel 4, 1989–94), *Birds of a Feather* (BBC1, 1989–98), *Keeping up Appearances* (BBC1, 1990–5) and *One Foot in the Grave* that were located in recognisably realistic settings, many of the more adventurous shows of the 80s and 90s had significantly non-naturalistic elements: the emotional and interpersonal dynamics of *The Young Ones* (1982–4), *Blackadder*, *Red Dwarf* (1988–9) and *Father Ted* (1995–8) might have been familiar but their worlds were heightened or alien. Even mainstream shows like *Goodnight Sweetheart* (BBC1, 1993–9) and *My Hero* (BBC1, 2000–) had an element of the fantastic at their core (time travel and superheroism respectively). Part of the appeal of *The Office* was arguably its novelty in presenting an environment that closely reflected the actual experience of many of its viewers – something that neither sitcom nor the other conventionally realist genre, soap opera, had been especially interested in at that time, the latter pursuing explosive crisis and celebrity casting rather than engaged naturalism or comforting banality.

Merchant says of soap opera that 'they burned up all the realism early on so now they have to constantly bring in gunmen and rape and whatever else.' Gervais adds that

There's also so much [hype] around soap opera now that it's hard to suspend disbelief because you know that she's actually pregnant or she doesn't want to be there or she's been in the paper that day saying 'I hate fucking Dirty Den'. Whereas [previously] you turned on *Coronation Street* and you were looking into your neighbour's house and they had great characters like Elsie Tanner and Minnie Caldwell and Albert Tatlock. These were your nan and granddad and they acted like them as well.

130 Like *The Royle Family*'s domestic scene, the workplace environment of *The Office* offered an identifiable experience absent from much comedy and soap output. Atalla recalls thinking that with *The Office*

People are feeling like somebody's gone out and made a comedy directly for them. Somebody has bothered at the BBC, this remote institution to most people, and made a comedy that's about my world, you know – I have to live with my mum, I work to earn money for Friday night, I'm not gonna be running ICI, I'm in a relationship with a childhood sweetheart that's not set my world alight but it's comfortable. This is my lot, I can see that.

The contemporary workplace

Certainly, *The Office* was unusually credible for its ostensible type. A viewer sitting down in July 2001 to watch a new BBC comedy set in an office could justifiably have had certain expectations. Full of complex farcical mishap, the conventional sitcom office is a pretty wacky place, at least in comparison with the likely professional experiences of viewers with clerical jobs. The models of exaggerated clerical drudgery were established with such early sitcoms as *Citizen James* (1960–2) and *Here's Harry* (1960–5) and had been in place long enough to have been semi-parodied in 1976 by *The Fall and Rise of Reginald Perrin* – a highly sophisticated series that still found room for admin-related cock-ups and farting chairs. This template remained current a quarter of a century on: *Kiss Me Kate* (1998–2000), *The Creatives* (1998–2000), *Chambers* (2000–1), *Perfect World* (2000–1), *Beast* (2000–1), *Black Books* (2000–4) and *High Stakes* (2001) were all set in workplaces and founded, some more successfully than others, on the traditional model of high jinks and high farce. Four months before David Brent's low-key first appearance, you could have tuned in to *Office Gossip*, a short-lived BBC1 sitcom featuring Pauline Quirke as beleaguered PA Jo, repeatedly grappling with inaccurate rumours of an affair with her boss Rod, and Neil Stuke as Simon, constantly trying to disguise an actual affair with manager Maxine. In a typical week, Jo might misguidedly convince Rod to pose as her husband to facilitate a car purchase, or Simon would pretend to be a gay wheelchair-user to put Maxine's husband off the scent. Not exactly your average day in the office.

By contrast, *The Office* offered an all-too-plausible reflection of the contemporary office environment; when David Brent chirps of the accounts department 'They are absolutely mad, all of them' (I.i) and gets blank, painfully sane stares in response, we know that, however desperately he tries to cultivate an air of wacky abandon, there will be no heightened office larks here. Wernham Hogg, it soon became clear, was not the sort of place where stationery cupboards frequently doubled as hiding places. Brent's own pathetic attempts at deception are generally rumbled embarrassingly quickly rather than forming the basis of episode-long intrigues.

Smaller humour was obviously in tune with the series' realism – given the pains gone to to achieve a convincingly banal milieu, it would have been incongruous to deliver too many OTT gags. More than this, though, it would have been incompatible with the emotional heft the series achieved over its fourteen episodes, much of which was dependent on viewers' investment in a recognisable situation. This depended not just on a familiar physical environment or the resonance of the docusoap form, important though these were: it was the series' implicit understanding of and response to the genuine frustrations and anxieties of the workplace at the turn of the century. Atalla notes *The Office*'s rejection of 'crazy offices' or glamorous media workplaces in favour of 'the office that people would recognise, the office of tedium, the office of the suburbs. I think there is quite a big streak of melancholy that runs through a lot of people's professional lives because … most people don't probably end up doing what they dreamt of as a kid.'

Few, certainly, would dream of a job at Wernham Hogg. We have seen how, in pursuit of a plausible docusoap aesthetic, the production was careful to do everything possible to attain formal realism, the location itself being the prime example. But where docusoaps would seize any opportunity to glamorise their subject matter, to present banal incident as gripping narrative, the environment of Wernham Hogg is designed to be as dull as it is possible to get away with. Gervais claims that 'a lot of people say that drama is real life with the boring bits taken out. Well, we made an issue of the boring bits.' Merchant confirms that 'It was an attempt to make people think: "This is what it's really like." ' From the plughole of the opening credits to the naturalistically artificial lighting and decor, the palette rarely strays beyond blues, greys and browns; Gareth's beige-and-taupe wardrobe in particular seems the open-plan equivalent of jungle camouflage, enabling him to blend in with the putty-coloured furnishings. The few flashes of colour that disrupt the drab inevitably prove disappointing

(Tim's outsized birthday present turns out to be an inflatable cock, Neil and Rachel's dance the opportunity for Brent's self-mortification).

The muted, deliberately unobtrusive yet quietly draining cutaways, set to the ambient chatter and hum of background conversation, mechanical operation and unanswered telephones, are one of the programme's most efficient means of conveying the genuine experience of the contemporary office. It's impossible to wholly separate the physical from the psychological experience of work, and many of *The Office*'s sharpest hits come from its attention to the open-plan design which has become a near-ubiquitous feature of the white-collar workplace. The model has grown in popularity over the past four decades because of its promise of a cheap, flexible and efficient environment where resources are shared and communication and supervision facilitated.[40]

Research into the effects of the approach, however, has not always yielded positive results: *The Office*'s ambient noise – distinctive and diverting but not always consciously noticeable – illustrates research findings that 'office noise distraction, even at the realistic level of 55 dBA, increases fatigue and has many negative effects on the performance of office work'.[41] Another assessment concluded that

> Environmental satisfaction decreased in open-plan offices as compared to traditional offices . . . Although these offices were designed to enhance communication, conversation noise is said to be quite distracting and typically irrelevant to the job. In addition, people find it distracting when others are moving and walking around them. Moreover, open-plan offices lack privacy in comparison to traditional office designs . . . so personal conversations, meetings with supervisors, errors or embarrassing behaviours might be seen or heard by co-workers.[42]

This could be a blueprint for the humour of *The Office*. One of the base notes of its comedy is the unwelcome, unavoidable interruption that underlines the absence of privacy – and, by extension, individual control – in the open-plan office. This trope is firmly established in the first series with Gareth's noisy tinkering with a Tipp-Ex dispenser or paper shredder and his and Tim's territorial squabbling over desk space; Dawn is especially badly afflicted, having to endure Donna's tactless relationship advice and Brent's creepy sidling up to discuss 'cancer of them old testicles' in I.i, having a good rummage right at her face level as she tries to enjoy a bit of Brie. (There's an especially antagonising edge to the interruption of eating; one of the series' few oases of calm comes in I.iv when we glimpse training-day moderator Rowan simply eating his lunch while reading a newspaper.) The second series opens with another such visitation – the chanting of the Muppet song around Tim's desk – and frequently revisits the mode, with the novelty cookie jar and 'Dirty Bertie' toy forming a constant aural assault.

The possibility of combining an invasion of aural privacy with tremendous scope for personal embarrassment is provided by that other

Brent has a rummage (I.i)

bane of open-plan life, the speakerphone. When Brent pretends to sack Chris Finch in I.ii or Gareth tries to show off his new conquest in II.vi, their attempts to use the public nature of the open-plan office to broadcast their authority or sexual prowess backfire in precisely the nature suggested by the report quoted above. The appearance in II.iv of computer technician Simon at Tim's computer ('It's not *your* computer, is it? It's Wernham Hogg's computer') presents another aggravating invasion. Most invasive is the imposition of Comic Relief day on the office in II.v, when any remaining vestiges of individual privacy are – according to Brent *et al.* – rendered forfeit in the coercive name of fun-in-a-good-cause. Thus one employee can be stripped of trousers and underwear not just in front of colleagues but in front of the camera and nation – a particularly neat illustration of how perfectly the eavesdropping docusoap style suits the open-plan environment, in which surveillance and self-consciousness are par for the course. Vulnerable to observation of various kinds throughout the day, the modern office worker quickly learns to conduct particular phone calls partly for the benefit of colleagues within earshot or time them to coincide with the absence of a superior; to avoid committing certain thoughts to emails that could be accessed by company administrators; to hold delicate conversations only in spots that are not part of the general thoroughfare. If it's not quite the Panopticon of Jeremy Bentham – although certain office designs come close – neither is the typical workplace so very distant from the kind of persistent scrutiny under which Brent so haplessly labours.

135

Of course, the enervative potential of the contemporary office is not simply a matter of physical environment. At a basic level, *The Office* rehearses complaints about the stifling frustrations of jobbing work – particularly bureaucratic or clerical work – that have been made throughout modernity. The first episode's opening scenes apparently establish the sort of open-ended, ennui-prone professional environment familiar to dissatisfied workers from Bartleby to Perrin: Brent announces he's been at Wernham Hogg for eight years, Dawn has 'been with us for ages, haven't you?', and Tim's job is so stale 'I'm boring

Wernham Hogg floor plan

myself talking about it'. But these impressions of interminability are undermined within a few minutes of this opening episode by the visit from head office's Jennifer Taylor Clarke in which the likelihood of job losses is established. Before we have even got the measure of the present situation we learn that it is jeopardised – a situation alien to viewers of conventional sitcom, but one increasingly common to real-life experiences of work. *The Office* effectively tapped into the double-bind of contemporary corporate employment: although there is nothing to alleviate the traditional frustration with a mundane, repetitive workload, this is now offset by fundamentally insecure job status; not only is the work unsatisfying, it could at any moment be lost to downsizing, streamlining, re-engineering or any other profit-maximising euphemism. This paradoxical meshing of ennui and anxiety is neatly summed up by an exchange in the film *Office Space*:

> **Peter:** What if we're still doing this when we're fifty?
>
> **Samir:** It would be good to have that kind of job security.

Tim and Dawn's apparent nonchalance at the prospect of redundancy notwithstanding ('I actually don't give a monkey's, do you?' she asks in I.i; 'I couldn't give a shit,' he concurs), their vulnerability, like every other employee's, is written on the situation from the start – a vulnerability that is subtly reiterated by the mock sackings that conclude the first two episodes (I.i with Brent's prank at Dawn's expense, I.ii with his faked dismissal of Chris Finch, which follows his claim to have made a non-existent employee redundant) and builds over the course of the first series to become the basis of the considerable suspense that hangs over its final episode. Merchant maintains that 'the redundancy thing was slightly arbitrary – we weren't trying to skewer Blair's Britain. It was a pure MacGuffin, but you need some sort of jeopardy'; if this is so, he and Gervais happened upon a form of jeopardy with tremendous resonance. As the narrator observes in John Lanchester's novel *Mr Phillips*, which follows a middle-aged accountant's aimless wanderings on the Monday after he has been made redundant, 'the world looks different, more fragile, when you have in mind that everyone everywhere tries to employ as few people as possible'.[43]

137

It's striking too that this is an internally imposed risk: the office is not threatened by a rival operation but placed in direct competition with another part of Wernham Hogg; we learn nothing about the company's wider fortunes beyond Jennifer's report in I.i that 'The board have decided that we can't justify a Swindon branch and a Slough branch.' Although in many ways *The Office* comes across as quintessentially British, this basic condition is common to the globalised economy exported from the United States – 'the fountainhead of market capitalism', as management theorist Charles Handy puts it.[44] The NBC remake of *The Office* is subtitled 'An American Workplace' but, in economic terms at least, Wernham Hogg is already an American workplace, in which corporate competitivity goes hand in hand with individual insecurity. In *The Corrosion of Character*, his book about the effects of such market practices on the worker's sense of identity and worth, Richard Sennett notes that

> What's peculiar about uncertainty today is that it exists without any
> looming historical disaster; instead it is woven into the everyday
> practices of a vigorous capitalism. Instability is meant to be normal,
> Schumpeter's entrepreneur served up as an ideal Everyman. Perhaps
> the corroding of character is an inevitable consequence.[45]

Ideas of the job for life or of companies privileging their staff's welfare
above their profits (or 'shareholder value') are now essentially quaint
ones; correspondingly, the individual's first duty becomes to him or
herself – and part of that duty is often to keep an eye out for favourable
opportunities and act upon them, even if it's not in the interests of others
around you: as Sennett puts it, '"No long term" is a principle which
corrodes trust, loyalty and mutual commitment.'[46]

Sloppy power structures

138   Whether it's reasonable to hold late-capitalist economic practice
responsible for David Brent being a prat is perhaps debatable, but he is
certainly well adjusted to the need to look out for number one. In his
own clumsy way, he merely represents endemic corporate doublespeak,
personifying the attempt to express sympathetic empathy while in fact
pursuing self-interest. Utterly incapable of negotiating the line between
pastoral care for and respectful distance from his staff, his behaviour
fluctuates, often on a dime, between presumptuous paternalism and
offhand dismissiveness, sometimes managing both at the same time:
when Malcolm seeks assurance of job security, Brent pats his head
Benny Hill-style rather than engaging with his concerns. Of his
manifold hypocrisies, the most pertinent is a faculty for demonstrating
breathtaking, if not always effectual, selfishness while trumpeting his
passionate defence of the welfare of his staff – his 'family', as he
repeatedly calls them. The moment Jennifer raises the issue of
redundancy in I.i, Brent struggles to convey both the compassion he
suspects to be ethically appropriate and the clear-headed business

sense he hopes will suggest an edge over his as yet unseen rival manager, Neil: 'I'm very concerned about redundancies, although I do understand if they are absolutely necessary, as a businessman, then they have to be – Does he understand if they're –?' In the next episode, Jennifer reacts with horror to Brent's declaration that he has assured staff that there will be no losses, suggesting that his professed aim of maintaining morale will surely be undermined if redundancies do in fact occur. After a beat, he waves his hand towards the outer office: 'They won't remember,' he assures her, contemptuously dismissive even as he tries to maintain an air of paternalistic benevolence. And when he is in fact offered a promotion at the end of the series – one whose acceptance would precipitate the Slough branch's closure – he again tries to slap the fig-leaf of pastoral care over his naked ambition. 'There is the emotion-as-good-in-business syndrome, sure,' he tells Jennifer when she wonders if his commitment to his staff might outweigh his desire for advancement, 'notwithstanding the cruel to be kind scenario.' (The jargon of management-speak, with its stream of abstract nouns and dynamic-sounding neologisms, suits Brent's evasiveness to a tee. 'We had to make the point that this man was using it as a shield,' Gervais says. 'He didn't really know about this sort of stuff, and when it actually came to the real training day he knew nothing. He was guessing – he just wanted to be the centre of attention.')

139

In many ways, then, Brent is in tune with the nature of the contemporary workplace. The problem is that although when it comes to his own career he acts with the recognition that loyalty and trust are of limited use, he still makes them the basis of his claim to managerial authority. When his initial assurance to his staff that 'no one is going to lose their jobs' is, reasonably, challenged as being beyond his capacity to guarantee, his response rests on the presumption of trust: 'I have promised it, okay, and it insults me that you even have to ask.' Even after it is established that redundancies are indeed a possibility, Brent offers an ultimatum that in effect comprises his total commitment to his staff:

Brent: Right, this is my ship and I am asking you to trust me and you can't go wrong.

Malcolm: Oh, David, it's not a question of trust.

Brent: It *is* a question of trust, Malcolm. Yeah, yeah, it is a question of trust.

Malcolm: It's communication –

Brent: Do you trust me? Do you trust me? Yes or no?

Malcolm: Yes, I trust you.

Brent: He does, so – Meeting adjourned.

In fact, Brent uses the notion of trust as a lever to avoid confrontation or taking responsibility. The flipside of his (failed) aspiration to put fun on the same footing as productivity – in I.i Brent assures Ricky the temp that he is 'a friend first, a boss second and probably an entertainer third', promptly debasing all three notions with his fake sacking of Dawn – is a readiness to shrug off the duties expected of a responsible boss. He does so by taking advantage of another typical facet of the modern workplace: the more relaxed approach to power structures that has accompanied the rise of the open-plan layout. Where conventional post-war management models retained a hierarchical and interpersonal formality operating along a somewhat military dynamic with clearly delineated 'ranks' of personnel, the desire to free up communication has yielded a less rigid structure characterised by first name terms and even an implicit parity of status: the boss as first among equals ... almost. Although this might seem to work to the benefit of employees, the sloppiness of the resulting hierarchy often yields opportunities for exploitation: Sennett notes that 'The new order substitutes new controls rather than simply abolishing the rules of the past – but these new controls are also hard to understand. The new capitalism is an often illegible regime of power.'[47] As we have seen, Brent's humour can itself be read as an index of this: Joe Moran observes that 'In the absence of a clear chain of command, the right to joke, and the compulsion to find something funny, mark out the invisible but resilient hierarchies of the office.'[48]

Perhaps the most conspicuous means by which Brent seeks to achieve self-serving dodges in this new, sloppy structure is the notion of 'teamwork'. In II.iii, Brent tries to impress Neil by claiming to be following a novel approach. 'I call it "team individuality". It's a new, it's like a management style. Again, guilty – unorthodox. Sue me.' He's evidently engaged his mouth rather than his brain, but 'team individuality' is probably as good a euphemism for this approach as any: while Brent routinely extols the notion of 'teamwork' he remains dedicated to his own welfare rather than that of his 'teammates'. In this Brent is hardly unusual (or 'unorthodox'), but simply subscribing in his own clumsy way to a now-commonplace fallacy – what Sennett describes as 'the fiction that workers and management are on the same team'. By adopting such a tactic, Sennett suggests,

> The boss avoids being held responsible for his or her actions; it's all on the player's shoulders. To put this more formally, power is present in the superficial scenes of teamwork, but authority is absent. An authority figure is someone who takes responsibility for the power he or she wields. In an old-style work hierarchy, the boss might do that by overtly declaring, 'I have the power, I know what's best, obey me.' Modern management techniques seek to escape from the 'authoritarian' aspect of such declarations, but in the process they manage to escape as well from being held responsible for their acts. 'People need to recognize we are all contingent workers in one form or another,' says a manager at ATT during a recent spate of downsizing; 'We are all victims of time and place.' If 'change' is the responsible agent, if everybody is a 'victim,' then authority vanishes, for no one can be held accountable – certainly not this manager letting people go.[49]

141

Back at the beginning of I.i, Brent made a great meal out of presenting
the forklift truck driver job he found for Alex as within his personal gift,
an index of his powerful individual status; when the time comes to take
it away, however, he insists it's 'out of my hands'.

> **Brent:** Do you think I enjoy doing this? This has been imposed upon
> me.
>
> **Alex:** 'This has been imposed upon me', 'This has been imposed upon
> me'.
>
> **Brent:** Yeah, it has. What do you want me to say? 'Oh, I'm sorry'?
> That'll give you your job back.
>
> **Alex:** Yeah. Yeah, I want you to apologise and stop passing the buck!
>
> **Brent:** I'm not passing the buck. This is someone else's decision. I
> didn't want to do this. You know, go above my head if you don't believe
> me . . .

142

For Brent, teamwork (or 'trust', or 'family') means never having to say
you're sorry, being able to pass the buck on anything from the disposal
of a fax from head office to Tim's dissatisfaction with his job; after
vigorously simulating sex with members of the Corrs in II.iii he even
turns to Neil and says: 'Your fault, putting filth in people's minds.' The
disingenuous blurring of the line between the interests of managers and
those of employees meshes all too neatly with Brent's tactless
presumption that others will share his privileging of his own interests:
'There's good news and bad news,' he tells staff at the end of I.vi – the
good news being his promotion, the bad their sacking or redeployment.
(Little wonder the BBC advertises *The Office* for use in management
training, claiming it 'offers everyday office situations presented in
heightened and exaggerated manner, providing trainers uniquely
poignant and funny metaphors for bad management. The next time a
manager says "It was only a joke" or "I like to be tough", show them
David Brent and they'll quickly see the problems in their approach.')

Job losses notwithstanding, the character who suffers most from the fallacy of teamwork is Gareth. Whereas Brent (cack-handedly) embraces informality and Tim and Dawn are frustratingly aware of the grim reality of their position, Gareth remains a throwback to the outmoded quasi-military structures of earlier management models, dependent on firmly delineated hierarchies and codified discipline, resentful of casualness and finding a way to view every situation as comparable to a field operation. 'It's all right here,' he says in a talking head in I.i,

> but people do sometimes take advantage because it's so relaxed. You know, I like to have a laugh just as much as the next man but this is a place of work. You know, I was in the Territorial Army for three years and you can't muck about there. That's sort of one of the rules.

For Gareth, security and confidence at work come from formal positions, discipline and a dependable chain of command, his place in which he jealously guards: he thrives on his titles of 'assistant regional manager' and 'team leader', impervious to Brent's constant correcting of the former ('assistant *to* the regional manager') and Tim's plausible insistence in II.i that

143

> 'Team leader' doesn't mean anything, mate . . . it's a title someone's given you to get you to do something they don't want to do for free, right? It's like making the div kid at school milk monitor. No one respects it.

Thanks to the opacity of this power structure, however, Gareth can persist in insisting that, for instance, he has the power to sack other employees without being authoritatively corrected. Meanwhile he eagerly pursues opportunities to impose punishment on recalcitrant colleagues and snaps up gobbets of perceived enhancement – when given use of the meeting room to investigate the pornographic joke email in I.ii he immediately establishes 'I can say to people: "Come into my office." '

His ethos of 'showing respect by obeying the law' (I.v) also applies to fun – on Comic Relief day in II.v Tim can easily goad him by forcing him to stick to his own rules ('Gareth's stopped hopping, everyone!') – and romance, obeying Brent's warning to stay away from Donna and later complaining to Ricky that 'I've played by the rules 'cause she was out of bounds. You nipped in behind everyone's back.' (I.v) He greets Tim and Dawn's eventual kiss in the second Christmas Special with 'Careful, she's got a fiancé'.

Apart from the opportunities for ridiculous chauvinism, hypocrisy and self-aggrandisement it affords, such a stickling approach is patently out of step with modern work practices. Gareth has a vague notion that informality is valued in the new workplace but can only pay it the clumsiest lip service ('Don't think of me as a boss,' he tells Donna in I.ii, 'but know that I am') and has no facility for the sort of 'soft' power which such informality in fact renders invaluable – a nose for opportunities, an ear for gossip. Despite considering himself Brent's

The old team on the scrapheap (I.vi)

privileged number two, Gareth is always last with the news (about the possibility of redundancy, about Brent's promotion) and worst equipped to adapt to changing circumstances; when Brent abandons his staff in I.vi, all are disappointed but only Gareth is surprised. Yet while his presumptions of loyalty, trust and consistency do him no favours, they are precisely the qualities whose absence makes the contemporary workplace a harsher, more corrosive environment, offering a degree of redemptive sincerity to his otherwise enervating actions. Although no less ridiculous, Gareth acquires a new sympathy during his tearful confrontation with Brent in I.vi, when we realise how seriously he takes both his own commitment to work and Brent's hollow assurances of trust and teamwork, whose undermining seems to matter more to him than the unmentioned threat to his own job:

Gareth: So you're definitely leaving then?

Brent: Yeah, it would appear so.

Gareth: What about us?

Brent [to camera]: There's nothing going on between us!

Gareth [to camera]: Not like that.

Brent: Not like that, no.

Gareth: You know, but we're a team. I'm assistant regional manager.

Brent: Assistant *to* the regional manager.

Gareth: So I can still be your assistant, can I? You know, if you're going off, then?

Brent: No, I'll be getting a proper assistant. A PA, God bless her.

Gareth: What, a lady?

Brent: Hopefully, yeah. Well, not 'cause of that, just –

Gareth: What about Neil? Is he going to be needing a –? I could be his assistant.

145

Brent: Neil's bringing his man with him. Bloody good guy, actually, good assistant. Bloke called Terry someone. You'd like him, he's ex-army.

Gareth: Territorial?

Brent: . . . No.

Gareth [choked]: Regular?

[Brent nods]

Gareth [panicked]: What rank?

Brent: Sergeant, I think.

Gareth: Pah.

Brent: What are you?

Gareth: Lieutenant, sir.

Brent: Anyway –

Gareth [almost in tears]: Well, that's it then, is it? The old team on the scrapheap. It's all gone.

Brent [embarrassed]: Gareth, come on. You're a soldier, aren't you? Eh? Yeah? Stiff upper lip and all that, eh? Spirit of the Dam Busters, yeah? A squadron never dies, does it?

Regardless of how misjudged Gareth's emotional commitment and application of a military model to a contemporary office might be, the spectacle of their collapse can't help but be affecting; hard too not to sympathise with the sentiment (if not the bitter pomposity) of his assertion later that episode that 'I work hard, I earn my keep. But unfortunately the history books are full of just people who toil and fight for worthy causes and the freedom of others.'

If Gareth's jobsworthy pedantry makes him the office's most grating employee, it also renders him most vulnerable to its vagaries. Still, every dog has its day and – thanks to Tim's reluctance to commit to an unenticing career ladder – Gareth ends up managing the Slough branch. His talking heads in the Christmas Special make clear that

> I did learn a lot from David. I learned from his mistakes . . . He used humour where I use discipline and I learned that nobody respected him. And in a war situation, if you want your platoon to go over the top with you to certain death, it's no good saying to them: 'Please come with me lads, I'll tell you a joke.'

Shared by no other employee, Gareth's approach brings more frustrations for both him and his staff and ultimately little more respect than Brent garnered ('Look at him! Look at his little boss face!' Tim taunts him at the Christmas party, having earlier locked him in his office).

Aspiration

Gareth's desire for advancement is not unusual: Brent's lust for glory as an entertainer becomes increasingly obvious over the course of the series, while the longing for a more challenging and rewarding professional life is one of the strongest links between Dawn and Tim; even Big Keith has hopes of becoming a DJ. Whereas aspiration has conventionally been seen as a somewhat exceptional quality – it forms the defining characteristic of many fictional heroes – in a professional context it is now relatively *de rigueur*. As Sennett observes, 'failure to move is taken as a sign of failure, stability seeming almost a living death . . . To stay put is to be left out.'[50]

The notion of progress as an inherent good is one that distinguishes modernity from earlier, essentially cyclical societies. Such movement is often more perceptible on a social than an individual level, but the importance placed on it is so pervasive that the individual who considers him or herself to be in stasis – 'in a rut' – often can't help but equate such a condition with personal weakness and failure.

Both the urge to move forward and the niggling self-doubt at failure to do so are present at Wernham Hogg. In the first series, Tim's hopes emerge as the most heartfelt, though they are not immediately obvious; while his dissatisfaction is plain, it is expressed through sarcastic humour – at his own expense as well as that of his colleagues and surroundings – rather than positive alternative strategies. His torpid self-deprecation is an understandable response to the frustrations of the workplace: unconvinced and unmotivated by cosmetic fictions like 'teamwork', Tim is typical of a type of disillusioned employee also identified by Sennett: 'In place of the driven man, there appears the ironic man ... An ironic view of oneself is the logical consequence of living in flexible time, without standards of authority and accountability.'[51] Yet, Sennett notes, Richard Rorty points out that irony does not enable you to challenge a situation, cannot make 'you better able to conquer the forces which are marshalled against you' but instead tends towards self-negation: "I am not quite real, my needs have no substance".'[52] Tim's self-deprecation is passive and ostensibly open-ended, his droll denigration of his circumstances sympathetic but unproductive – he seems detached from his own dissatisfaction, even when redundancy or promotion offers a potential prompt.

In I.vi, Dawn, similarly unhappy and similarly passive, expresses hope that redundancy might force her hand:

> I hope they get rid of me because then I might actually get off my arse and do something. I don't think it's many little girls' dream to be a receptionist. I don't know what I'll do but whatever it is it's got to be a career move and not just another arbitrary job. Tim's advice is that it's better to be at the bottom of a ladder you want to climb than halfway up one you don't. I just don't want to be treading water, you know, and then wake up in another five years' time and say: 'Shit, done it again.'

Tim similarly talks of 'an alarm clock [going] off'. To an extent, both regret their own inactivity, their choice to remain unsatisfied rather than hazard change. Dawn's announcement in I.iv that she's thinking of moving away provokes in Tim a similar reaction to the redundancies, its disruptive implications yielding a degree of anxiety but also potential liberation. In combination with the soul-numbing exercises of the training day, it proves the spur for his own transition from self-disparagement to action: the decision to go back to university to study psychology. In the end, the first series ends with the *status quo* maintained: Brent himself misses promotion by failing a medical; Dawn does not move away (yet); and, perhaps most disappointingly, Tim is seduced into staying – and adopting Brent's nonsense-speak about 'looking at the whole pie' – by a token promotion and minimal pay rise. The reinforcement of stability is not, here, a happy ending but rather a downbeat, depressing one – it offers not the restoration of equilibrium but the denial of improvement.

(The exception to this trend is Ricky, the temp. Youngest staff member and bottom of the office pecking order, he is also the best educated – not only a graduate but one who 'scraped a First' (I.i) – and the object of envy for his relationship with Donna. This tension has been the source of conflict with Brent and Finch, but is now resolved because, Brent tells us, he's 'off pursuing his career'. As the first series ends, he alone seems able to escape the gravity of Wernham Hogg.)

Tim's new attitude, conscientious and self-defeating, persists through the early episodes of the second series; jarringly, he expresses jobsworthy punctiliousness towards Gareth and Dawn. Although he still mentions university as a vague prospect, his new perspective seems resigned rather than aspirational: 'I'm thirty – time to grow up, basically. It's that simple' (II.i). Growing up here seems to mean accepting an unsatisfactory situation for the sake of stability, abdicating the responsibility of risk associated with survival in a corporate landscape in which the support of institutions cannot be relied on. 'Not to gamble is to accept oneself in advance as a failure,' as Sennett puts it. 'Risk is a test of character: the important thing is to make the effort, take

149

the chance, even if you know *rationally* you are doomed to fail.'[53] This ethos is perhaps more applicable to the entrepreneur than the clerical worker, but it chimes perfectly with Tim's rationale for staying put (II.vi):

> If you look at life like rolling a dice then my situation now, as it stands – yeah, it may only be a three. If I jack that in now, go for something bigger and better, yep, I could easily roll a six, no problem. I could also roll a one, okay? So I think sometimes just leave the dice alone.

This retrenchment extends as far as declining internal promotion so as not to raise the stakes any further: Tim fears that if he accepts Neil's offer of Brent's former position he will find it even harder to leave Wernham Hogg; yet rather than quit altogether he simply remains in his current post. Dawn, on the other hand, does take the plunge and leaves with Lee for the US at the end of the second series, but the signs are that this change of scenery will not represent a qualitative improvement: rather than encouraging her aspirations as an illustrator, Lee expresses the hope that she 'gets a job on reception out there'; when we revisit them in Florida in the Christmas Special he boasts that 'our situation here is almost as good as it was in Slough'. Since Dawn's departure, Tim has evidently been growing ever more frustrated at Wernham Hogg, having merely swapped Brent's inane management for Gareth's. Dawn's return seems to spark his suppressed aspirationalism, if only by proxy: constrained by social decorum from raking over his romantic feelings, he expresses his concern for Dawn's welfare in a professional context. Her hopes of being an illustrator are repeatedly flagged up as the key issue of her return: before visiting the office, the 'director' asks why it has fallen by the wayside (her response is a Brentian stream of non-committal abstract nouns: 'Um, just circumstance, really ... 'cause of priorities and time and all that, really'); she discusses giving up art with Gareth when she arrives ('Good, good, waste of time') but is later seen doodling an impressive sketch of Tim. Art and aspiration, along with a sense of humour, are subtly established as the bonds that define Tim and Dawn's relationship as something apart from the other employees – and something lacking in her relationship with Lee, as shown in this exchange between the two men at the party:

> **Tim:** Hey, Lee, have a word with this one about not doing the old illustrating any more! I heard she's not drawing or painting –?
>
> **Lee:** No.
>
> **Tim:** Really? I'd have thought you had the perfect spot.
>
> **Lee:** Nah, we agreed, living's got to come first.
>
> **Tim:** But she could still do it in the evening, no?
>
> **Lee:** Yeah, but to make money out of it you've got to be good.

Persistence reaps rewards (Christmas Special, Part Two)

Taken aback, Tim keeps schtum, but his and Dawn's bond proves the more substantial: just as she confirmed it with the gift of the portrait sketch, he, clinchingly, gives her an art set with the ultra-aspirational message 'Never give up' – and it is this that ultimately persuades her to make the biggest leap of all and dump Lee for Tim.

Tim's continuing encouragement, even after the apparent fading of his own personal resolve, clearly impresses the like-minded Dawn. But Brent and Gareth are, for different reasons, disparaging of their aspirations from the start: to Gareth, who knows his place, Dawn's initial thoughts of leaving are 'just stupid – you've got a job here for life' (I.iv) (an outmoded notion *per se* but especially wrongheaded given the imminent likelihood of job losses at Wernham Hogg), while he dismissively asks Tim 'What you want to be a psychiatrist for? They're all mad themselves, aren't they?' (I.v) Brent's response is more complicated, informed by both knee-jerk denigration and his own insecurities; despite his assurance in his first ever speech that 'if a good man comes to me and says . . . 'I want to better myself, I want to move on", then I can make that dream come true'. He in fact consistently pooh-poohs the slightest sign of aspiration in any of his employees. Although presumably Tim and Dawn's desire to leave could alleviate the downsizing difficulties, Brent can't help but take it personally. Viewing Tim's dissatisfaction as an opportunity to solicit praise and demonstrate his supposed pastoral skills, he turns bitter when unable to dissuade him from his choice ('Go and do some work instead of whinging . . . You try and do a good deed . . .', I.v); Keith's ambitions become an excuse for Brent to show off about his own attempted musical career; and when, in II.ii, Dawn for the first time details her hopes of being an illustrator, he dismissively patronises her: 'Pipe dreams are good, in a way . . . if you keep trying, at least then when it doesn't happen, you can go: "At least I gave it a go." ' That 'when' says it all.

This stands in sharp contrast to his own avid self-promotion, both within Wernham Hogg in the first series and outside it later on.

152

Yet despite the hypocrisy of his self-interest, Brent's working life is presented in such a way as to engender increasing sympathy for him. To start with he is smug and seigneurial, a bargain basement Godfather offering jobs here and there, comparing himself to Solomon and Jesus, shocked at Donna's having sex with Ricky because 'He's not even a permanent member of staff' (I.v). Despite lying to his superiors, he not only avoids the sack but is ultimately offered promotion, only to lose the opportunity because of high blood pressure. Brent's apparent imperviousness irked some viewers, and even producers, who felt such incompetence would surely go unrewarded. (Gervais and Merchant reasonably suggested a simple look around any workplace – including the BBC – would soon turn up managers at least as incompetent.) Yet in the second series the focus shifts from Brent as boss to Brent as employee: he is increasingly placed in the position of vulnerability associated in the first run with those under him. From the beginning, his managerial position is placed under new scrutiny, from below: the new intake from the defunct Swindon branch do not necessarily share the long-standing Slough employees' resigned tolerance of his 'fun' approach, challenging his delusions of success. In a group meeting in II.ii he is shocked by their attitude.

153

Trudy: We're actually used to doing stuff, like. Working hard, you know, being motivated. But there's not much dynamism out there, is there? I mean, people look like they're getting away with murder.

Brent: Having a laugh, yes.

Trudy: Well, I think quite a few of us are bored.

Most galling is the claim that, even though they don't share Brent's high premium on fun, the newcomers think Neil – their old boss and Brent's new superior – was 'more of a laugh' anyway. Returning later from a failed attempt to demonstrate his own entertainment value at a pub lunch, Brent is irked to find Neil overseeing a successful game of indoor cricket at the office. His petulant response earns him a stinging dressing down from Neil, adding opprobrium from above to the lack of confidence from below. The episode concludes with Brent imposing himself on Dawn for a self-pitying moan and, while we don't envy her situation, it's perhaps the first time we've been asked to feel sorry for Brent.

His insecurity becomes clearer over the course of the series, expressed through his hopeless rivalry with Neil for staff respect and even Chris Finch's friendship. It also becomes clear that his professional incompetence has not after all gone unnoticed: he is repeatedly reprimanded and eventually told by Neil that 'if you can't improve your margin and your volume sales, with or without making people laugh, if you can't do that, you and I are going to have to have a very serious chat' (II.iv). Ultimately Brent's hubris does him in: when, on Comic Relief day, Neil demands an overdue report, Brent makes a cocky, wounded aside suggesting they sack him and, tired of 'your consistent negligence and failure to do what is asked of you' (II.v), they take him up on the offer. That he is wearing a comedy ostrich suit provides a necessarily pathetic edge to what could otherwise be an unbearably awkward moment; here Brent's trademark self-delusion ('You are going to have a mutiny on your hands. They will go beserk. Definitely') takes on a touching bathos, as does the indifference with which his dismissal is greeted by the staff. Just as the last episode of the first series had Gareth on the verge of tears at the thought of losing his job, the second ends with Brent brimfully begging for his:

> I will try twice as hard, I really will. I know I've been complacent and I'll turn this place around if we just say that it's not definite now, and then we can, um – 'You're not going until –' Starting from now. Starting from now.

With this first sign of humility and willingness to change, not to mention such pitiful pleading, it's no longer possible to view Brent with simple

Starting from now (II.vi)

disdain; his transition from high-handed boss to impotent employee complete, it would be harsh to deny him sympathy even if his troubles are self-authored.

The character descends even further into pitiability in the Christmas Specials. In Lanchester's novel, Mr Phillips goes for a wander in the park, unsure what to do with himself. Another man approaches him and strikes up a conversation about worklife.

'You're a what?' asks the man in the park.
'I'm not anything now,' says Mr Phillips.
'That's no way to think.'
'But it's true.'[54]

Brent faces a similar quandary. It's made painfully obvious that, having no life to speak of, he has now made a habit of hanging around the Wernham Hogg offices for the sake of simple human contact, provoking demeaning exchanges with Gareth and Neil about his right to be there and eventually dependent on Tim's pity to avoid utter humiliation ('Yeah, I'll have a drink with you tomorrow, David,' he agrees, salvaging a scrap of Brent's dignity). The business instincts of which he was once so confident have repeatedly let him down: his sideline in motivational speaking came to nothing, his self-released single was a flop. We learn that, bereft of an institutional framework, his work portfolio now comprises two models of individualist entrepreneurialism, one prototypically old-fashioned and tied to peddling wares, the other quintessentially postmodern and concerned with the promotion of an insubstantial image: travelling salesman by day, jobbing micro-celebrity by night. Neither is going well. Brent seems able to shift units in the cleaning products trade but it's hardly lucrative, while his 'celebrity' appearances are embarrassing both for his desperate attempts to trade off while denying his reputation as 'that awful boss' (as a prospective date describes him) and for the vaguely hostile indifference with which his hollow attempts are met.

156

Ploughing up and down the motorway week in week out, Brent half-heartedly attempts to present his car as an 'office environment', but the constant shots of hard shoulders, service stations and semi-industrial nightspots underline his loneliness. In this he resembles Vincent, the lead in Laurent Cantet's film *L'Emploi du temps* (2001), another contemporary story about a downsized executive. Not telling his bourgeois family about the change in his circumstances, Vincent takes to hanging around offices and travel intersections – what Marcel Augé has called 'the non-places of supermodernity . . . spaces of circulation, communication and consumption, where solitudes co-exist without creating any social bond or even a social emotion'.[55] Cantet's description of Vincent's contradictory desires also seems apt to Brent's frustrations: 'There's a paradox between his desire to be elsewhere, to experience a certain precariousness, and his wish to preserve what brings him equilibrium . . . We saw the character as a scriptwriter who writes his own life, directs it

Time out (Christmas Special, Part Two)

and then plays it.'[56] Brent has always tried to write his own script – we have seen his attempts at shaping narrative through commentary and intervention – but his delusions are no longer tenable. After yet another soul-sapping public appearance, he wearily tells his agent 'I don't wanna do these any more', but can only look back, not forward, rehashing his old script rather than drafting a new one; drinking alone in his motel room he indulges pathetic fantasies of Wernham Hogg begging him to return, and their Christmas party represents a lone beacon of sociability. Impotent and pathetic, there's little to fear or even contemn now in 'the boss from hell'; yet redemption of a sort comes in the shape of Carol, his blind date. It's her ability to reframe Brent's current experiences into a different, positive narrative that lets us leave *The Office* feeling positive about Brent's emotional well-being, if not his career prospects:

Brent: . . . seems to be a series of shitty little PAs at the moment. You know, I go out and wave for ten minutes. Embarrassing. And they're all half me age and I know they're taking the mick, but –

Carol: Well, not really. You know, you're getting paid, you never see them again, what do you care? Take the money and run.

[Brent looks pleasantly surprised by this take on the situation.]

Carol: Spend it on something you do want to do.

Brent (nodding): Yeah.

Ultimately, Merchant and Gervais achieve a sense of hope for Brent by shifting his and our attention away from professional success – an area in which he seems unlikely ever to meet his own disproportionate expectations – and onto his personal life, specifically the prospect of a relationship. As we leave *The Office* it's with the feeling that, for all their annoyances and hardships, jobs aren't worth getting too worked up about.

158

The old gang (Christmas Special, Part Two)

An American workplace

The same is not always true for workers in the United States, where an employer can exert a far greater impact on their staff's quality of life than is usual in northern Europe. *The Office*'s attention to workplace anxieties was perhaps one of the reasons for its transatlantic success. When BBC America (the Corporation's entertainment channel in the US) first broadcast the series in January 2003, it received a wide range of positive reviews laced with concern that the show might prove too subtle for general audiences: the *Los Angeles Times*, for instance, asked readers to 'Imagine a television series about mid-level workers stuck in dead-end jobs. Now imagine producing it without big stars, laugh tracks, tidy endings or glamour ... It sounds, well, un-American, doesn't it?'[57] While it's certainly true that *The Office*'s aesthetic was more alien to mainstream US sitcom than it had been to British viewers – especially those familiar with, say, *I'm Alan Partridge* or *The Royle Family* – it was hardly unAmerican: as we have seen, Gervais and Merchant took most of their inspiration from US output, from Billy Wilder to Woody Allen, *This Is Spinal Tap* to *The Larry Sanders Show*.

The show performed well on BBC America, but this hardly made it a household name: a digital channel available to a minority of US viewers, BBCA could be pleased with ratings of 350,000, whereas a top-rated episode of *Friends* would attract almost a hundred times as many viewers. But as *The Office*'s domestic progression had shown, initial ratings were a limited index of success. A year after its initial transmission, on 25 January 2004, the series unexpectedly won two Golden Globe awards, which are chosen by the Hollywood Foreign Press Association: it

Stephen Merchant, Lucy Davis, Martin Freeman, Ricky Gervais and Ash Atalla at the Golden Globes – looking, in Gervais' words, 'like something you'd paid a shilling to see in a tent a hundred years ago'

beat *Sex and the City* (1998–2004) and *Will & Grace* (1998–2006) in the best comedy series category while Gervais won best comedy actor over *Will & Grace*'s Eric McCormack and *Friends*' Matt LeBlanc. As the first British show even to be nominated for the awards (it was eligible only because of BBCA's nominal contribution to the second series' budget), expectations of *The Office* had been so low that the cast were instructed to linger on the red carpet in the hope of being photographed on the way in and cameras were not even trained on their table during the announcement of the results. If few present had even heard of the series, its wins secured it significant capital. Even before BBCA began transmission of the series, discussions had been underway regarding an American adaptation of the show, and in August 2003, Greg Daniels, co-creator of the animated sitcom *King of the Hill*, had confirmed that his company Reveille was developing the property, dubbed *The Office – An*

American Workplace. Within a week of the Golden Globes, a cast was announced and pre-production started on a pilot to be screened on the NBC network. The result would yield three big surprises: first, how closely it cleaved to the original series; second, how successful this new context proved to be; and third, the fact that, despite mediocre ratings, NBC defied industry norms and commissioned another season.

The American pilot episode inevitably incorporated changes to the format to take account of its relocation – 'Nothing ever changes by staying the same,' as David Brent once observed (II.iii) – but its most striking attribute was its fidelity to the BBC template. Wernham Hogg of Slough became Dunder-Mifflin of Scranton, Pennsylvania; David Brent, who quotes 'The Two Ronnies', became Michael Scott (Steve Carell), who loves 'The Three Stooges'; Tim, Dawn and Territorial Army veteran Gareth were redrafted as Jim, Pam and volunteer Sheriff Deputy Dwight. To those familiar with the original, the slightly broader performances of beloved set-ups could not help but jar, but this underlined how little else had changed: the faux-documentary shooting style was no slicker, the

161

An American workplace

Dwight (Rainn Wilson) and Jim (John Krasinski)

setting no more glamorous, the characters no more ingratiating; there were still no one-liners, no laugh track, no lessons learned; there were still desperate appeals to the camera; it still ended with grim, anticlimactic deflation rather than peppy affirmation. Even on a cable station such as HBO, which had produced *Larry Sanders*, this approach might have been considered challenging; on a major network like NBC – home of *Friends* and *Frasier* – it was unprecedented. Despite highly equivocal reactions to the pilot, NBC retained faith in the project and commissioned a further five episodes. Since the demise of both its flagship sitcoms in 2004, the network had struggled to find popular replacements; it is possible that this motivated it to be more adventurous in its commissioning practices.

The new episodes, broadcast from March 2005, maintained the original series' formal approach but departed from Gervais and Merchant's scripts. The show nevertheless proved well suited to its new setting, not least because many of the workplace anxieties that *The Office* tapped into result from economic practices that originated in America; in the US the consequences of having a negligent manager are potentially graver than in the UK, and therefore have more comic potential. As well as the threat of redundancy and their boss's crass jokes and boorish insensitivity, Michael Scott's employees have to deal with his mishandled downgrading of their health insurance and cavalier decision to commit them to weekend working; comparably, where Gareth's officiousness irritates Tim, Dwight's costs Jim a deal that accounts for twenty-five per cent of his annual income. Perhaps even bolder is the series' transference of Brent's unreconstructed prejudices, finding humour in the area of racism, usually taboo for mainstream US sitcoms. Michael makes cringeworthy attempts at 'black' slang and at one point asks Mexican–American employee, Oscar: 'Is there a term besides "Mexican" that you prefer? Something less offensive?' Unsurprisingly for the network that triumphantly folded continuing romantic narrative into sitcom with *Friends* and *Frasier*, NBC's *Office* also accelerated the rapport between Jim and Pam, but without sentimentalising it: we learn much earlier, for instance, of Jim's admiration for Pam's art; she also proved to be more proactive in instigating pranks at Dwight's expense than Dawn had been, a refreshing variation on Dawn's generally passive characterisation. There's attention too to television as subject matter, not just in Michael's quotations but in character behaviour explicitly modelled on reality formats such as *Survivor* (Dwight's attitude to downsizing) and MTV's *Punk'd* (Michael's practical jokes).

163

Reviews were generally – if reluctantly – positive: 'Though it grates to admit it,' said the *New York Times*, the show 'is funnier than any other new network sitcom'; *Time* magazine praised its 'daring, unflinching take on very American workplace tensions'. Initially promising ratings dwindled over the six-episode run, which would usually consign a new comedy to cancellation, but the network announced 'we could not face the prospect of not bringing it back given the history NBC has had with the likes of *Seinfeld*' – a show whose unlikeable characters and plots 'about nothing' initially alienated audiences before making it one of the most successful sitcoms in history. At the time of writing it remains to be seen whether *The Office – An American Workplace* will be able to emulate that show's success; that

NBC should take the chance at least suggests a relatively bold willingness to experiment with genre on the network's part. If the new version does catch on, it could be at the expense of its characters. Where Gervais and Merchant were able to structure a linear narrative that ultimately delivered change and relief for Tim, Dawn and David Brent, it's hard to see how such resolution would be compatible with the institutional demands of a successful US network sitcom, conventionally expected to produce dozens of episodes a year for as long as remains viable. The more popular Jim, Pam and Michael Scott prove to be with American audiences, the less likely they are to get what their British counterparts so arduously earned: a happy ending.

Notes

1 Michael Leapman, 'As the BBC's Comedy Department Faces Crisis. Is This the End for TV Sitcoms?', *Daily Mail*, 30 May 2001.

2 Dominic Cavendish, 'Private View', *Daily Telegraph*, 3 June 2001.

3 Vanessa Thorpe, 'Both Feet in the Grave', *Guardian*, 3 June 2001.

4 Purves told an anecdote in which the producer of a series he had worked on told him there was 'good news and bad news': the programme had been given the go-ahead for a second series, but Purves was being dropped. This was adapted into Brent's address to his staff after his own promotion in I.vi. Purves himself presented the corporate video seen in I.iv.

5 Stirling Gallacher, who would later play David Brent's boss Jennifer Taylor Clarke.

6 Documentary, *The Office* series one DVD bonus material.

7 Documentary, *The Office* series one DVD bonus material.

8 'Sitting', from the album *Catch Bull at Four*. Gervais and Merchant also suggested the track for use on the NBC remake of *The Office* (which instead used Electric Light Orchestra's 'Mr Blue Sky'), and themselves used another Cat Stevens track – 'Tea for the Tillerman' – as the theme for *Extras*.

9 The line runs: 'It's like sitting in a barber chair. They're going to ask me: "You got anything to say?" and I say: "Sure. Give me a haircut, a shave and a massage."'

10 Dovey, 1.

11 Dovey, 1.

12 Corner, 256.

13 Brenton and Cohen, 36.

14 Beattie, 191.

15 Dovey, 139.

16 Beattie, 194, ref. G. Ballfante, 'Their So-called Lives', *Time*, 31 July 1995.

17 Mapplebeck, 25.

18 Dovey, 152.

19 Dovey, 136.

20 'Kicking up a Storm', *Broadcast*, 26 March 1999.

21 Clark, 13.

22 See Gillan.

23 Posted 7 September 2003 at <www.tvforum.co.uk/forum/viewtopic.php?t=6347&highlight=]>

24 Biressi and Nunn, 111.

25 At the end of one of my own interviews with Gervais, he made a tongue-in-cheek request regarding representation of his answers: 'If you could just tighten mine up, make it a lot more articulate, and do it like I said it without all the 'ums' and 'ahs'. Can't make me pretentious, anything too waffly. Um, anything that's incorrect.' In another discussion of his and Merchant's follow-up series, in pre-production at the time, he offered the following: 'If this [book] goes out after *Extras* went out, it was a lush and beautifully observed follow-up to *The Office*. If anything it was an improvement

on some of the characters and double Golden Globe-winner Gervais, if possible, improved on the performance of David Brent with Andy Millman.'

26 Corner, 263.

27 The trope is more bathetically echoed in the desperate looks Sheila can occasionally be seen throwing at Oliver in the Christmas Specials following her shy declaration in II.vi that 'I like blacks' – a whole mini-story played out in glances as she gazes over at him and is then reduced to tears when he gets off with Trudy.

28 Clark, 9.

29 Moran, 47.

30 Bowes, 129.

31 Eaton, Wollacott and McQueen respectively.

32 Episode 1F14, 'Homer Loves Flanders'.

33 Neale and Krutnik, 281–1.

34 Crowther and Pinfold, 64.

35 'The Little Kicks', episode 138.

36 Goddard, 75.

37 Lovell, 28.

38 Koseluk, 7.

39 Tim Devlin, 'The Making of *Dad's Army*', *The Times*, 26 December 1973.

40 Joe Moran observes that 'the Wernham-Hogg office is a variation on *Bürolandschaft*

[office landscaping], a concept developed in the late 1950s by the German management consultants, Quickborner, and popularized in English-speaking countries in the 1960s by the architect and designer Francis Duffy.' Moran, 43.

41 *International Journal of Indoor Air Quality and Climate Study*, Witterseh *et al.*

42 The National Research Council of Canada, Duval *et al.*, 4.

43 Lanchester, 80.

44 Author interview.

45 Richard Sennett, *The Corrosion of Character*, 31.

46 Sennett, 24.

47 Sennett, 10.

48 Moran, 43.

49 Sennett, 113–5.

50 Sennett, 87.

51 Sennett, 115.

52 Sennett, 116.

53 Sennett, 90.

54 Lanchester, 72.

55 Vincendeau, 30.

56 Vincendeau, 32.

57 Gary Younge, 'Office Intrigue Attracts the US Networks', *Guardian*, 24 January 2003.

Episode Guide

I.i

January 2001. David Brent welcomes a documentary crew to the Slough branch of Wernham Hogg paper merchants, where he has been general manager for eight years. After employees Dawn, Tim and Gareth have been introduced, Jennifer Taylor Clarke arrives from Head Office to announce that either the Slough or the Swindon branch will soon be closed, with inevitable redundancies. At an office meeting Brent assures the staff their jobs are safe. Meanwhile, recent graduate Ricky starts work as a temp, Tim angers Gareth by setting his stapler inside a jelly and Brent 'sacks' Dawn in a misjudged practical joke that ends in tears.

I.ii

Donna, daughter of friends of Brent, begins work experience, prompting showing off among the male staff. A digital composite of Brent's face on a pornographic picture is circulated on the office email; he charges Gareth with uncovering the culprit. Jennifer arrives and tours the warehouse with Brent – an awkward encounter during which his self-serving deception becomes obvious. Gareth accuses Tim of making the image but Tim identifies Brent's friend Chris Finch as the real culprit. Jennifer suggests Brent sack Finch, which he appears to do over the phone; when Jennifer clicks on the speakerphone, however, we hear the speaking clock.

I.iii

It's Tim's thirtieth birthday. Dawn warmly congratulates him but Brent is more concerned about the annual quiz night that evening – though he delightedly uses one of Tim's presents, a giant inflatable cock, as a prop for 'improv' comedy. Quizmaster Gareth prepares the questions, which turn out to be largely military-themed. Reigning champs Brent and Finch tie with Tim and Ricky (who has appeared on *Blockbusters*); Ricky beats Finch in a tie-breaker but later the losers claim victory by succeeding in throwing Tim's shoes over the building. Tim walks home in his socks.

I.iv
Staff-training expert Rowan comes into the office for a day of exercises, though Brent finds it impossible to relinquish centre stage. Dawn and her fiancé Lee are arguing; Tim comforts her. In the training session, the staff watch a video, do some role-playing and discuss motivation, all of which Brent hijacks and scuppers by showing off. Rowan's frustration increases when Brent gets his guitar and starts singing songs from his days as a musician. After lunch a similar pattern emerges. Eventually Tim snaps, announces he's quitting and asks Dawn out. She tells him she and Lee are reconciled.

I.v
Tim describes his plans to take a psychology degree; he and Dawn are awkward in one another's company. Donna arrives late; it turns out she has slept with someone from the office. Brent interviews two candidates to be his PA: Stuart gets short shrift but he sleazily coos over Karen. Having given her the job and invited her to Chasers nightclub that evening, Brent accidentally headbutts her. Gareth clumsily tries to pump Donna for information about her sex life. At Chasers that night Donna reveals that she has been seeing Ricky and Brent artlessly flirts with Karen. Gareth goes home with a married couple.

I.vi
Brent begins sacking staff as Karen starts work, and tries to talk Tim out of quitting. Jennifer reports her own promotion and offers Brent her old position as UK manager, which would necessitate closing the Slough

branch. He agrees and tactlessly breaks the news that jobs will either be lost or relocated to Swindon. Gareth is very upset. At the end-of-year party that night, spirits are low until Brent announces that in fact the Slough branch will incorporate Swindon, preserving everyone's jobs. Rather than this being an act of magnanimity, it turns out Brent has failed his medical. To Dawn's disappointment, Tim has been tempted into staying by a small promotion.

II.i
Two weeks later. Tim has a new title and a new, jobsworthy attitude and remains distant with Dawn. Brent meets the new UK manager Neil, former manager of the Swindon branch, some of whose staff are joining the Slough office. At an induction meeting Neil charms the employees but Brent's attempts at humour go down badly, with one racist joke prompting a complaint to Jennifer. Newcomer Rachel attracts Tim's attention and the tension between him and Dawn thaws as they wind Gareth up together. Lee arrives to see them jokily dancing together and shoves Tim away.

II.ii
Lee apologises to Tim for shoving him. Brent carries out staff appraisals, getting irked by Tim's continued intention to return to university and Big Keith's unresponsiveness. During a fire drill Brent and Gareth leave Brenda, who uses a wheelchair, halfway down a stairwell and Tim flirts with Rachel, to Dawn's annoyance. Later Rachel asks him out for a drink. Hoping to improve relations with the newcomers Brent organises a pub lunch, which falls flat. He resentfully accuses Neil of courting popularity, prompting Neil to give him a dressing down, then expresses his frustrations to Dawn.

II.iii
It's newcomer Trudy's birthday; one of her gifts is a pink dildo, which Rachel challenges Tim to secrete in Brent's office. He succeeds, making both Dawn and Gareth jealous of their fun. Tim gives the newcomers a

tour of the warehouse, whose staff crack offensive jokes. Training
consultants Ray and Jude arrive and ask Brent to lead a motivation
session, despite his uncovering the dildo as they talk. Rachel and Dawn
both try to engage Tim in further pranks. At Trudy's birthday drinks
Brent abortively flirts with Trudy and makes crass jokes and comments.
Later she and Finch have sex in the car park.

II.iv
Rachel and Tim kiss in the corridor, to Dawn's mortification. Brent
prepares for his motivational training session, although Neil is
concerned it might detract from his office work. IT engineer Simon
works on Tim's computer and tells implausibly self-aggrandising
anecdotes. Brent is angered first to find staff have been ridiculing his
weight and then to receive another telling-off from Neil. Dawn
accompanies Brent to his speaking session as his assistant. He is
childishly excited to be 'backstage' and fails to notice how badly his
session goes, leaving on a high while Dawn clears up after him.

II.v
It's Comic Relief day. Brent wears a red nose, Gareth has to hop all day
and Dawn is selling kisses for a pound. Neil and Rachel steal the show
with a *Saturday Night Fever*-style dance routine, which Brent promptly
follows with an improvised and indescribably bad dance of his own.
Brent has a meeting with Jennifer and Neil, who gives him a warning for
his negligence; Brent angrily challenges Neil to sack him. Tim buys a kiss
from Dawn, which both find disquieting. Neil tells Brent he is indeed
sacked; Brent announces this to the unresponsive staff dressed in an
ostrich costume in preparation for a photo shoot with the local paper,
which he, Tim and Dawn pose for in drab humour.

II.vi
Brent puts a brave face on his imminent departure, showing off the fact
that trade journalist Helena has arrived to interview him for an article.
Tim turns down Neil's offer to stand in as Brent's replacement, suggesting

Gareth instead. Having been distant with Rachel, Tim breaks up with her, pleading with Gareth not to try to comfort her. In front of Helena, Ray and Jude tell Brent they don't want any more work from him. He throws all three out. Tim is disturbed to learn that Dawn is leaving for the US with Lee and again tells her of his romantic interest. She rejects him. Brent begs Neil and Jennifer for his job but is also refused.

Christmas Special (Part One)
December 2003. Brent, resentful of his depiction in the documentary, is now a travelling salesman by day and a jobbing micro-celebrity by night. We see the video to his self-financed single, which flopped. He still regularly visits Wernham Hogg, where Gareth has taken over his job. Tim still plays pranks on Gareth but misses Dawn's company. She and Lee are still in Florida, but accept the TV crew's offer to fly them home for the Wernham Hogg Christmas party. Brent is invited but challenged by Neil and Finch to bring a date; Gareth helps him subscribe to an internet dating service. Brent takes part in a 'celebrity' *Blind Date*-style nightclub show, which goes disastrously.

171

Christmas Special (Part Two)
Brent has two dates from the internet service, both of which go badly. Dawn nervously arrives at the office for a visit; Tim is apprehensive too but they are pleased to see each other. Her unrealised aspiration to be an illustrator is mentioned. Trudy sets up a 'Secret Santa' scheme for staff to buy each other presents. When Brent comes to the office with his dog Neil bans him from unannounced visits. He is also fed up with nightclub appearances. At the party Lee downplays Dawn's aspirations to be an illustrator. Brent is pleasantly surprised to find his blind date, Carol, attractive and sympathetic. Eventually Lee tells Dawn they're leaving; she collects her 'Secret Santa' gift and opens it in the cab to find a painting set from Tim with a note saying 'Never give up'. Carol leaves, hoping to see Brent again. Newly confident, he tells Neil and Finch to 'fuck off'. Dawn returns to the party having broken up with Lee. She and Tim kiss and a happy group photograph is taken.

Bibliography

Baker, James, *Teaching TV Sitcom* (London: BFI, 2003).

Beattie, Keith, *Documentary Screens: Non-fiction Film and Television* (Basingstoke: Palgrave Macmillan, 2004).

Bennett, T., S. Boyd-Bowman, C. Mercer and J. Woollacott (eds), *Popular Television and Film* (London: BFI/Open University Press, 1981).

Bennett, T., C. Mercer and J. Woollacott (eds), *Popular Culture and Social Relations* (Milton Keynes: Open University Press, 1986).

Biressi, Anita and Heather Nunn, *Reality TV: Realism and Revolution* (London: Wallflower Press, 2005).

Bowes, Mick, 'Only When I Laugh', in Andrew Goodwin and Garry Whannel (eds), *Understanding Television* (London and New York: Routledge, 1990), pp. 128–40.

Brenton, Sam and Reuben Cohen, *Shooting People: Adventures in Reality TV* (London: Verso, 2003).

Bruzzi, Stella, 'Docusoaps', in Glen Creeber (ed.), *The Television Genre Book* (London: BFI, 2001), pp. 132–4.

Buscombe, Edward (ed.), *British Television: A Reader* (Oxford: Oxford University Press, 2000).

Casey, Bernadette, Neil Casey, Ben Calvert, Liam French and Justin Lewis (eds), *Television Studies: The Key Concepts* (London and New York: Routledge, 2002).

Clark, Bernard 'The Box of Tricks', in Dolan Cummings (ed.), *Reality*

TV: How Real Is Real? (London: Hodder & Stoughton, 2002), pp. 1–16.

Cook, Jim (ed.), *BFI Dossier 17: Television Sitcom* (London: BFI, 1982).

Cook, Jim, 'Narrative, Comedy, Character and Performance', in Jim Cook, *BFI Dossier 17: Television Sitcom* (London: BFI, 1982), pp. 13–18.

Corner, John (ed.), *Popular Television in Britain* (London: BFI, 1991).

Corner, John, 'Performing the Real: Documentary Diversions', *Television and New Media* 3 (3) (California, 2002), pp. 255–69.

Corner, John and Sylvia Harvey (eds), *Television Times: A Reader* (London: Arnold, 1996).

Creeber, Glen (ed.), *The Television Genre Book* (London: BFI, 2001).

Crowther, Bruce and Mike Pinfold, *Bring Me Laughter: Four Decades of Television Comedy* (London: Columbus Books, 1987).

Cummings, Dolan (ed.), *Reality TV: How Real Is Real?* (London: Hodder & Stoughton, 2002).

Curtis, Barry, 'Aspects of Sitcom', in Jim Cook (ed.), *BFI Dossier 17: Television Sitcom* (London: BFI, 1982), pp. 4–12.

Dovey, Jon, *Freakshow: First Person Media and Factual Television* (London: Pluto Press, 2000).

Duval, Cara L., Kate E. Charles and Jennifer E. Veitch, 'Open-Plan Office Density and Environmental Satisfaction', National Research Council of Canada Research Report RR–150, 27 September 2002.

Eaton, Mick, 'Television Situation Comedy', *Screen* vol. 19 no. 4 (1978), reprinted in Bennett *et al.*, *Popular Television and Film* (London: BFI/Open University Press, 1981).

Gillan, Jennifer, 'From Ozzie Nelson to Ozzy Osbourne: The Genesis and Development of the Reality (Star) Sitcom', in Su Holmes and Deborah Jermyn (eds), *Understanding Reality Television* (London and New York: Routledge, 2004), pp. 54–70.

Goddard, Peter, '*Hancock's Half-Hour*: A Watershed in British Television Comedy', in John Corner (ed.), *Popular Television in Britain* (London: BFI, 1991), pp. 75–89.

Goodwin, Andrew and Garry Whannel (eds), *Understanding Television* (London and New York: Routledge, 1990).

Hill, Annette, 'Crime and Crisis: British Reality TV in Action', in Edward Buscombe (ed.), *British Television: A Reader* (Oxford: Oxford University Press, 2000), pp. 218–34.

Holmes, Su, '"All You've Got to Worry about Is the Task, Having a Cup of Tea, and Doing a Bit of Sunbathing": Approaching Celebrity in *Big Brother*', in Su Holmes and Deborah Jermyn (eds), *Understanding Reality Television* (London and New York: Routledge, 2004), pp. 111–35.

Holmes, Su and Deborah Jermyn (eds), *Understanding Reality Television* (London and New York: Routledge, 2004).

Koseluk, Gregory, *Great Brit-Coms: British Television Situation Comedy* (Jefferson, NC: McFarland, 2000).

Lanchester, John, *Mr Phillips* (New York: G. P. Putnam, 2000).

Lovell, Terry, 'A Genre of Social Disruption?', in Jim Cook (ed.), *BFI Dossier 17: Television Sitcom* (London: BFI, 1982), pp. 19–31.

Mapplebeck, Victoria, 'Money Shot', in Dolan Cummings (ed.), *Reality TV: How Real Is Real?* (London: Hodder & Stoughton, 2002), pp. 17–34.

McQueen, David, *Television: A Media Student's Guide* (London and New York: Arnold, 1998).

Medhurst, Andy and Lucy Tuck, 'Situation Comedy and Stereotyping', in John Corner and Sylvia Harvey (eds), *Television Times: A Reader* (London: Arnold, 1996).

Moran, Joe, *Reading the Everyday* (London and New York: Routledge, 2005).

Neale, Steve and Frank Krutnik (eds), *Popular Film and Television Comedy* (London and New York: Routledge, 1990).

Roscoe, Jane, 'Real Entertainment: New factual Hybrid Television', *Media International Australia* 100 (Brisbane, August 2001), pp. 9–20.

Thompson, Ben, *Sunshine on Putty: The Golden Age of British Comedy from Vic Reeves to* The Office (London and New York: Fourth Estate, 2004).

Vincendeau, Ginette, 'White Collar Blues', *Sight and Sound*, April 2002, pp. 30–2.

Webber, Richard, *The Life and Legacy of Reginald Perrin: A Celebration* (London: Virgin, 1996).

Witterseh, Thomas, David P. Wyon and Geo Clausen, 'The Effects of Moderate Heat Stress and Open-plan Office Noise Distraction on SBS Symptoms and on the Performance of Office Work', *Indoor Air* vol. 14 no. 8, December 2004, pp. 30–41.

Woollacott, Janet, 'Fictions and Ideologies: The Case of Situation Comedy', in Bennett *et al.* (eds), *Popular Culture and Social Relations* (Milton Keynes: Open University Press, 1986).

175

Credits

The Office
Series One
United Kingdom/2001
written and directed by
Ricky Gervais
Stephen Merchant
producer
Ash Atalla
director of photography
Andy Hollis
production designer
Julie Harris
editor
Nigel Williams
title music arranged by
Big George
©/production company
BBC
executive producers
Anil Gupta
[BBC] Jon Plowman
production manager
Gail Evans
production co-ordinator
Linda Hearn
programme finance associate
Debbie Somerville
production executive
Sarah Hitchcock
location manager
Tracy Jane Read
assistant directors
1st: Jo Randall
2nd: Rob Smith
3rd: Zac Thraves
script supervisor
Caroline Gardener
casting director
Rachel Freck
camera operators
Richard Farish
Conor Connelly [2–6]
camera assistant
Rupert Burton
gaffer
Paul Barlow
art director
Jane Fredericks
props master
Matt Wyles
costume designer

Sarah Higbid
wardrobe supervisor
Rose Goodheart [Goodhart]
make-up designer
Lucy Cain
make-up artist
Val Akrill
sound recordist
Mark Found
boom operator
James Judge
dubbing mixer
Andrew Sears
cast
Ricky Gervais
David Brent
Martin Freeman
Tim Canterbury
Mackenzie Crook
Gareth Keenan
Lucy Davis
Dawn Tinsley
Oliver Chris
Ricky Howard
Stirling Gallacher
Jennifer Taylor Clarke
with
Joel Beckett
Lee
Robin Hooper
Malcolm
Paul Sharma
Sanj
Yvonne D'Alpra
Joan
Neil Fitzmaurice [1/6]
Alex
Sally Bretton [2–6]
Donna
David Schaal [2]
Glynn
Ralph Ineson [3/5]
Chris 'Finchy' Finch
Vincent Franklin [4]
Rowan
Peter Purves [4]
Peter Purves
Nicola Cotter [5–6]
Karen
Robin Ince [5]
Stuart Foot

Ron Merchant [6]
office janitor
and
Ben Bradshaw
Ben
Angela Clerkin
Jackie
Jamie Deeks
Jamie
Jane Lucas
Sheila 'Mouse'
Ewen MacIntosh
Keith Bishop
Emma (Louise) Manton
Emma
Alexander Perkins
Ralph
Philip Pickard
Phillip
Richard Hollis [4]
Lucy O'Connell [4]
Ellen Collier [5]
Kiki Kendrik [5]
Tiffany Stevenson-Oake [5]
Dick Bradnum [6]
1) BBC2 tx 09/07/2001
(29m 39s)
2) BBC2 tx 16/07/2001
(29m 4s)
3) BBC2 tx 23/07/2001
(29m 20s)
4) BBC2 tx 30/07/2001
(29m 7s)
5) BBC2 tx 13/08/2001
(29m 28s)
6) BBC2 tx 20/08/2001
(29m 10s)
Although there are no on-
screen titles, series one
episodes have been given the
following titles in various
sources:
1) Downsize, 2) Work
Experience, 3) The Quiz,
4) Training, 5) New Girl,
6) Judgement.

The Office
Series Two
United Kingdom/2002
written and directed by

Ricky Gervais
Stephen Merchant
producer
Ash Atalla
director of photography
Andy Hollis
editor
Nigel Williams
production designer
Julie Harris
title music arranged by
Big George
©/production company
BBC
executive producers
Anil Gupta
[BBC] Jon Plowman
production manager
Jane Sprague
production co-ordinator
Sarah Rose
programme finance associate
Jackie Byrne
production executive
Sarah Hitchcock
location manager
Tony Boucher [2–5]
production runner
Lucy Fewell
assistant directors
1st: Steve Roberts
2nd: Rob Smith
script supervisor
Emma John
casting directors
Tracey Gillham
Rachel Freck
camera operator
Drew Seymour
camera assistant
Ben Robinson
art director
Alex Merchant
props master
Simon Blackmore
costume designer
Sarah Higbid
wardrobe supervisor
Rose Goodheart
wardrobe assistant
Tabitha Doyle
make-up designer
Lucy Cain
make-up artist
Kate Roberts

choreographer
Carol Fletcher [5]
sound recordist
Mark Found
boom operator
James Judge
sound assistants
Kate Harris
Julian Bale [4–6]
dubbing mixer
Glenn Calder
cast
Ricky Gervais
David Brent
Martin Freeman
Tim Canterbury
Mackenzie Crook
Gareth Keenan
Lucy Davis
Dawn Tinsley
Patrick Baladi
Neil Godwin
Stacey Roca
Rachel
with
Stirling Gallacher [1/5/6]
Jennifer Taylor Clarke
Joel Beckett
Lee
Julie Fernandez
Brenda
Rachel Isaac
Trudy
Ewen MacIntosh [1–3/5/6]
Keith
Howard Saddler
Oliver
Ralph Ineson [3/5]
Chris 'Finchy' Finch
Tom Goodman-Hill [3/4/6]
Ray
Jennifer Hennesey [3/4/6]
Jude
David Schaal [3]
Glynn
Matthew Holness [4]
Simon
Che Walker [4]
speaker 1
Richard Wills-Cotton [4]
speaker 2
Hugh Parker [5]
photographer
Bruce Mackinnon [5]
Jimmy the Perv

Stephen Merchant [5]
Nathan, 'The Oggmonster'
Olivia Colman [6]
Helena
Jamie Deeks
Jamie
and
Ben Bradshaw
Ben
Patrick Driver
Patrick
Jane Lucas
Sheila 'Mouse'
Tony MacMurray
Tony
Emma (Louise) Manton
Emma
Alexander Perkins
Ralph
Philip Pickard
Philip
Peter Heppelthwaite [3]
Sue Gifford [4]
Ron Merchant [6]
office janitor
1) BBC2 tx 30/09/2002
(29m 11s)
2) BBC2 tx 07/10/2002
(29m 19s)
3) BBC2 tx 14/10/2002
(29m 4s)
4) BBC2 tx 21/10/2002
(29m 11s)
5) BBC2 tx 28/10/2002
(28m 56s)
6) BBC2 tx 04/11/2002
(29m 1s)

The Christmas Specials
United Kingdom/2003
written and directed by
Ricky Gervais
Stephen Merchant
producer
Ash Atalla
director of photography
Andy Hollis
editor
Nigel Williams
production designer
Alex Craig
title music arranged by
Big George
©/production company
BBC

177

178

executive producers
Anil Gupta
[BBC] Jon Plowman
production manager
Paul Williams
assistant production manager
Ian Locker
production co-ordinator
Grace Boylan
finance associate
Kelley James
production executive
Sarah Hitchcock
location manager
Scott Sidey
runner
Alison Marlow
assistant directors
1st: Steve Roberts
2nd: Rob Smith
3rd: Kieran Baine
script supervisor
Emma John
casting
Tracey Gillham
Jo Buckingham
Rachel Freck
camera operator
Drew Seymour
camera assistant
Ben Robinson
art director
Alex Merchant
production buyer
Charlie Sammons
props master
Jo Vinton
costume designer
Sarah Higbid
wardrobe supervisor
Tabitha Doyle
dresser
Emily Wilson
make-up designer
Lucy Cain
make-up artist
Kate Roberts

Brent's single arranged by
Glyn Hughes [1]
sound recordist
Mark Found
boom operators
James Judge
Kate Harris
dubbing mixer
Glenn Calder
cast
Ricky Gervais
David Brent
Martin Freeman
Tim Canterbury
Mackenzie Crook
Gareth Keenan
Lucy Davis
Dawn Tinsley
Patrick Baladi
Neil Godwin
Elizabeth Berrington
Anne
with
Ralph Ineson
Chris 'Finchy' Finch
Joel Beckett
Lee
Ewen MacIntosh
Keith
Steve Brody
Pete, David's agent
Sandy Hendrickse [2]
Carol
and
Howard Brown [1]
Greg Burns [1]
Alec Christie [1–2]
Paul ['Bubble'] Ferguson [1]
Mike McClean [1]
Sandy McDade [1–2]
Robert Purdy [1]
Kellie Shirley [1]
Renton Skinner [1]
Ash Varrez [1]
Rebecca Charles [2]
JoAnn Condon [2]
Julia Davis [2]

voice of Gillian
Cally Lawrence [2]
David Schaal [2]
Glynn
with
Ben Bradshaw
Ben
Jamie Deeks
Jamie
Julie Fernandez
Brenda
Ben Forster
Martha Howe-Douglas
Rachel Isaac
Trudy
Emma (Louise) Manton
Emma
Jane Lucas
Sheila 'Mouse'
Alexander Perkins
Ralph
Philip Pickard
Philip
Howard Saddler
Oliver
[*uncredited*]
Bella
Nelson the dog
1) BBC1 tx 26/12/2003
(43m 33s)
2) BBC1 tx 27/12/2003
(51m 51s)
title music [uncredited]
Handbags and Gladrags
composed by Michael D'Abo,
performed by Fin with Ben
Hallett (drums), Del
Bromham (guitar), Whibble
(piano), Snake Davis (soprano
sax). Ricky Gervais/David
Brent performs the track over
the end credits of series one,
episode four.
Credits compiled by Julian
Grainger.

Acknowledgments

With thanks to Rob White for the opportunity to write this book and much valuable advice; Rebecca Barden, Tom Cabot, Sophia Contento and Zoe Drayson at BFI Publishing; the staff of the BFI Library and National Film and Television Archive; Ash Atalla, Ricky Gervais, Anil Gupta, Stephen Merchant, Jon Plowman and Jane Root; Duncan Hayes and Lisa Toogood; UKTV; Charles Handy, for a very useful conversation about work culture; Nick James, Edward Lawrenson and Phil Wickham at the BFI and also Matthew Bright, Neville Gomes, Alex Goodall, Andrew Harrop, Patrick Higgins, Chris Hogg, Michael Shaw, Anthony Szynkaruk and JM Tyree, whose suggestions improved the book; and, as always, my family.

Index

Page numbers in **bold** indicate detailed analysis; those in *italic* refer to illustrations. *n* = endnote.